LIVING BOUNTIFULLY!

LIVING BOUNTIFULLY!

The Blessings of Responsible Stewardship

LINDA H. HOLLIES

THE PILGRIM PRESS CLEVELAND

DEDICATION

This book is dedicated to the memory of my youngest son,

GRELON RENAURD EVERETT, AKA PEANUT

Sunrise: AUGUST 29, 1963
Sunset: MARCH 27, 2004

The Pilgrim Press, 700 Prospect Avenue, Cleveland, Ohio 44115-1100
thepilgrimpress.com
© 2005 by Linda H. Hollies

10   09   08   5   4   3   2

Library of Congress Cataloging-in-Publication Data

Hollies, Linda H.
       Living bountifully : the blessings of responsible stewardship / Linda H. Hollies.
       p.   cm.
       Includes bibliographical references.
       ISBN 0-8298-1676-3 (pbk. : alk. paper)
       1. Stewardship, Christian.   2. Christian women—Religious life.
3. African American women—Religious life.   I. Title.

BV772.H583   2005
248'.6—dc22
                                                      2005041926

CONTENTS

Contents

PREFACE

For almost three years, I have experienced living on God's bountiful love and grace. For almost three years, I have watched God perform the miracles of ancient days on my behalf. For almost three years, I have been the beneficiary of God's amazing grace far beyond what I ever thought, expected, or anticipated.

Life has presented me with some difficult challenges in the past three years. Life has made me aware that we cannot dictate, figure out, or even be prepared for the unexpected events that turn our world upside down. Many of you recall the little bird Chippie from my book *Jesus and Those Bodacious Women: Life Lessons from One Sister to Another.* Well, over the course of the past three years, I have become Chippie!

Almost three years ago, life sucked me up, washed me over and tried to blow me dry! First, I was "fired" from my conference staff consulting job and later appointed to a local congregation. I was then "fired" from the congregation by a former "friend," who happened to be my bishop. My good and steady income was gone. I was placed on disability leave, not wanting to recognize that I needed space to cry, to heal, and to reclaim my voice. Like that little bird Chippie, I couldn't sing much anymore! My joy was gone, as I had depended upon my roles in the church.

I know with certainty that my responsible stewardship paid off in this horrible period of my life. Life had been going so well until two years prior to that time—so well, that I had increased my tithe from 10 percent to 15 percent. I recognized that God had been more than gracious, more than kind, and more than generous on my behalf. And, as my "territory" increased and my income became greater, I felt it necessary to say "thank you" to God in a tangible manner.

For almost three years, my family and I have been the recipients of God's bountiful living program. Our needs have been provided for. God has proved a mighty good "booking agent" and my travels, my book writing, and my magazine assignments have increased. No! My income is not "regular." No! We have not won the lottery. No! We are not gambling at the casinos. But we have been, and are, depending on God, who continually provides. I am a witness to the promise of Malachi, to whom God declared that when we tithe: "See if I will not open the windows of heaven for you and pour down for you an overflowing blessing!" (Mal. 3:10).

Some years ago, I bought a purple sleep shirt that reads: "God is my source." I really didn't have a clue when I purchased that shirt that I would actually live by its declaration! But today, I am a living witness that God does continually provide. More importantly, I know that responsible stewardship does pay off! I had to learn that tithing is about more than my little 15 percent "tip" to God. Tithing is about me doing the very best that I can to wisely manage my entire life. I am, after all, steward over what I've been given from God.

We all need to recognize, acknowledge, and claim that we are recipients of God's amazing and bountiful benefits. Without God's welfare, the air that we take for granted would not flow through our nostrils and our lungs; the ability to think and to react would be gone; and the opportunities to care for ourselves, to worship, and to pray would not be ours. We are the owners of *nothing*! All that we have, all that we are, and all that we might potentially become, belongs to God. We are simply stewards being trusted by God!

The little known story in Numbers 27 of Mahlah, Noah, Hoglah, Milcah, and Tirzah, bold women who knew the Law, is the sort of tale that frees us to do the unheard of, never-been-done things in life! The tradition always favored the men—the sons in the family. But, their father, Zelophehad, had been a true follower of Moses and a true believer in God's faithfulness. There is a stewardship required of our lives, how we live ethically and whom we chose to follow.

When Korah and his followers attempted to overthrow the leadership of Moses, Zelophehad had stood with Moses in faithful and responsible stewardship. God honored their father by granting the women's request to own the land that had rightfully belonged to Zelophehad, who had no male heirs. The laws changed in Israel that day. God said, "It shall be for the Israelites a statute and ordinance " (Num. 27:11b). On that day, the women in Israel learned about the joyous benefits of living on the bountiful reform plan of God!

This book is about responsible stewardship in every area of our lives. This book is about how we can extract principles from the folks who have "been there, done that, and made it to the record book!" This book is about the freedom that we can experience, the lives that we can live, and the joyous enthusiasm that we can spread as we apply God's economic principles in our lives.

My purpose in life is to teach the people of God—utilizing the harsh and often difficult life lessons that I am forced to learn— through the medium of preaching, teaching, and writing. This book is simply a record of what I have researched and lived about the joy of God's welfare plan. This book will share with you how God made a way out of no way when I couldn't see, imagine, or figure out a method to keep my sanity, my sobriety, or my salvation. I can write today, with joy! My economic worldview has been transformed. I am a better, more responsible steward of what God provides.

Even now I am praying with and for you. I so want you to experience and to trust the advent of grace in your life. I so want you to appreciate the full benefits of joyfully living on God's welfare reform plan. This book will transform your thinking, challenge your way of life, and offer you options to consider as we grow in more responsible stewardship, together.

Some of the things that we read in Holy Scripture sound so foolish to our contemporary ears. Some of the things recorded in Holy Scriptures don't make good, practical sense according to the "me first" way that we live. Some of the things that we read and discover in the Living Word of God seem so far fetched from our "normal" customs and traditions.

The mystery of God's ways, however, is a big part of our faith journey. And, in order to live with joy and on God's bountiful benefit plan, we just might have to do things in "strange" ways. Don't spend loads of time worrying about the "how" that God uses. Just begin to anticipate all the wonderful results that we are seeking and will discern! It's promised! On the journey with you—Shalom!

In every book that I've written, a sista-friend has ministered unto us a poem that has been written as she journeyed through her painful season on her way to bountiful living. I offer you the ministry gift of poet Phenessa Gray.[1] Shalom!

—*Sista Linda*

I'M THROUGH CRYING!

I'm through crying,
and feeling the intense pain in the pit of my stomach,
and reaching for distant arms that aren't there,
and looking for the wind to answer unanswerable questions,

and talking to brick walls,
and screaming for the help that was inside of me all along,
and trying to please an unpleasable being,
and trying to measure up to standards beneath me,
and settling for less than I deserve.
I'm through crying,
and shaking from fear of being left,
for being left, abandoned, betrayed, lied to, forsaken,
violated, abused,
and trying to understand someone who doesn't understand
themselves,
and fearing being strong and assertive and determined and
all the things that make me who I am, a queen,
and compromising my royalty to an unfaithful subject for his
love that never existed in the first place,
and being tired,
and being tried,
and forsaking who I am, what I am and Whose I am,
and searching for a heart that has no heart at all.
I'm through crying,
and blaming myself,
and letting others blame me for something I didn't do,
and accepting the blame to carry the peace,
and wanting the blame so he can feel better about himself,
and compromising the blame to compromise myself to compromise
my heart, my soul, my body to someone who neither deserved
the thought, the energy, nor the sleepless nights, nor the
anxiety shivers, nor the anorexia, nor the depression, nor
wails of "What did I do???"
and prolonging the inevitable ending of two people, on
different levels,
on different plains, on different planets, on different

capacities, on different, different, different.
I'm through crying,
for nothing,
who is nothing,
what is nothing,
nothing from nothing leaving nothing,
for the nothing he gave,
for the nothing promises he spoke,
for the nothing support he administered,
for the "I love yous" he knew nothing about,
for the nothing love he couldn't give because he only read
about it in books and saw it on television—a worldly love,
so common, so overused,
so outdated, so quickly distorted, so instantly said, so much
full of nothing.
I'm through crying,
and forgetting who I am,
and forsaking who I am,
and letting him tell me what he claimed was wrong with me,
and letting him insult me, belittle me, tear me down,
and accepting his mental, spiritual, and emotional abuse.
Lord, God, Creator, forgive me for placing an insignificant
man in front of you,
and tolerating someone who was intolerable,
and being a good woman to someone who doesn't deserve me,
and overexerting my love to the limits and destructive
expectations of his cruelty,
and giving all of myself to someone who couldn't appreciate a
morsel, let alone deserve a limb of my kindness, my care, my
compassion, my passion, my goodness, my patience, my
long-suffering, my unconditional love, my favor.
I'm through crying!

ACKNOWLEDGMENTS

So that, with the eyes of your heart enlightened, you may
know what is the hope to which he has called you, what are the
riches of his glorious inheritance among the saints, and what is the
immeasurable greatness of his power for us who believe,
according to the working of his great power.

—EPHESIANS 1:18–19

These pages are to acknowledge more of the vast and wonderful network of folks who have touched my life and shared their love, care, prayers, and wise counsel with me. Several pages could not contain their names. An entire book could not hold their gifts to my life. Only eternity will be able to reveal my rich and glorious portion of kin, friend and family. I owe each one named untold gratitude.

This book is dedicated to my personal Responsible Stewards and Life Coaches! They include: Dr. Clifton Jones, Dr. James Abbington, and Mr. Tony McNeill of Friendship Missionary Baptist Church, Charlotte, North Carolina; Mama Doretha Robinson Adams, Big Mama Eunice Robinson Wade, and Granny Lucinda Robinson Weston, my life sources; Barbara Jean Baker Vinson-Van Buren, my bestest-sista friend; Darlene Sims Lee, and Elizabeth Clark Brown, my school years' "best friends"; Ms. Ethel Sims, Ms. Catherine Jones, and Aunt Sweetie, neighborhood "mothers"; Thelma Nunn Pryor and Madine Blakley; lifelong church sistas; Hortense House and Della Burt, teachers/mentors/friends; Emma Justes and Emilie Townes, seminary professors; role models JoClare Wilson and Cynthia Smitko; CPE (clinical pastoral education) guides and pushers Helen Marie Fannings Ammons and Marilyn Magee; "sista-mothers"/friends Linda Foster Mumson, Barbara Issacs, and Cecelia Long; North Illinois path clearers Ida Easley, Fran Brandon, and Brenda Heffner; seminary prayer group; Marie Antoinette Carson, great woman; good friends Vera Jo Eddington and Joyce E. Wallace; Twinkling Butterfly Club, Harlene Harden, Beverly J. Garvin, Vanessa Stephens-Lee, Cynthia Belt, LaSandra Dolberry, Connie Wilkerson, Carolyn Wilkins, and Juana Dunbar; Carolyn Abrams, who loves me unconditionally; Valerie Bridgeman Davis and Genevieve Brown, who were personal prophets in calling me to fly; Daisybelle Thomas Quinney and Janet Hopkins, sistas; Eleanor L. Miller, my pastor and intercessor; Lucille Brown, Ruby Earven, and Ray Margaret Jackson, surrogate mothers, sages, and bodacious women of wisdom.

A book is never written in isolation. All the persons who touch, influence, inspire, and even hinder your life help you in the writing process. The lessons you have learned and the individuals who taught you hover over your shoulders, waiting to see if you mastered the materials. In the same way that "it takes a village to raise a child," it takes your entire life community to write a book.

I'm thankful to my life community for my personal experiences and awareness of the journey of forgiveness. Many are the charitable and gracious souls who have forgiven me when I have stumbled, blundered, and just plain messed up! I have been picked up, lifted up, forgiven, and blessed to grow and to become by my life community.

My family of origin heads this list of folks who helped to write this book. My grandmothers—Lucinda Weston, Eunice Wade, Ethel Kellom, and Lessie Bell King—live in me, speak to me, and continue to admonish and cheer me as they watch from the realms of glory. My Big Daddy, Dock Wade, is with them and I appreciate the loving role modeling he provided. My parents, James and Doretha Adams, gave me life and granted me the necessary lessons that have taught me to hold on to God's unchanging hand! My aunt Barbara Weston taught me by example the art of meditation, relaxation, releasing, and letting go of yesterday's pain. My uncle, her spouse, Clenton Weston, taught me how to be there for family.

Finally, there is my father in ministry, Rev. James A. Anderson, who opened the doors to professional ministry to me. They all await me on the "other side." I simply pray that I teach their lessons of wisdom well. For, truly, they taught me with their lives.

My siblings and extended family are the rich soil that has nurtured my soul. For Jacqui, Bob, and Troy; Riene, Tony, Lynne, Michael, and Missy; Regina, Arthur, Raymond, Ibn, and Millicent; James Jr., Jeanette, Noah and Mohanna; Eddie, Onnette, Eddie Jr., and Candance; David, Kim, Dave Jr., and Ean; and Robert Tyrone and Lisa, I give God thanks and praise. Finally, my husband, Mista Chuck, is my soul-mate and best friend; my daughter, Grian Eunyke, her sons, Giraurd and Gamel, her daughter, Symphony; my sons, Gregory Raymond and Grelon Renard Everett, have each taught me lessons and learned because of me how to love and to forgive. My "family" is another name for Love! Chuck's children have included me and mine in their family circle over these thirty-plus years and Wisdom demands that I name them: Pam and Erin; JoAnne, Paul, Lacie, Cory, and Darian "Bear"; Donna, Ronald Charles, and Anita.

There are children of my womb and there are daughters of my heart: Angie Hooks, Jacqui Ford, Tracy Flaggs, Darlene Webster, and Sandy Adams. There are brothers who have helped me along life's winding road and made my life easier. These are Da Boys, my colleagues, brothers, and friends, who always have my back: Dr. Zawdie K. Abiade (and Nancy), Apostle Anthony Earl (and Rev. Bobbie), Dr. Michael Carson (and Rev. Katherine), Dr. Dennis Robinson (and Rev. Darlene), and Dr. Donald Guest (and Brenda).

I have some primary cheerleaders who pump me up and call me to write "on demand": Kim Martin Sadler, Linda Peavy, Rev. Marge, Phil and Azariah Bermann, and Rev. Cynthia Stewart. And I'm thankful to my copyeditor, Kris Firth, who keeps me honest! I have an awesome beautician, Pamela Tardy, who not only hooks up my hair and keeps the grey away, but also ministers to me with dazzling homemade quilted wall hangings.

These are the folks who are responsible for me being the bodacious, wise woman that I am today. I have been touched, impacted, and inspired by their lives. For each of them and more, I give God total praise! My prayer is that they, too, are always surrounded by Wisdom's counsel.

This book is dedicated to my son. Grelon Renaurd Everett was his given name to connect him with his older brother, Gregory Raymond, and to signify their great potential in life. The doctor who delivered him nicknamed him "Peanut" because of his little head and big eyes. Grelon was cremated at the age of forty after several years of having his physical temple ravaged by the effects of kidney failure caused by severe diabetes.

A Pizza Hut box was found in his kitchen, showing his disdain for following standard procedures and rules. We always said that Grelon walked to the beat of a different drummer; both tall and large in stature, he took band and then taught himself to play the flute professionally because he said he could hear angels singing to him. He shared his musical gift in so many different places. Over several days after his death, I was given the revelation for the disposition of his remains. Grelon's brother Gregory Everett, of Southfield, Michigan, and several male cousins (known as the "Posse") were given a gift box to be taken to several spots. Each one of them found their designated family member and/or place, said a prayer, and gave Grelon back to the care of one of our ancestors. Gregory visited Horace Mann High School and the family home where the children were raised in Gary, Indiana. His cousin Clenton Weston Jr. of Detroit, Michigan, took a gift box to their maternal great aunt, Aunt Eunice Wade, who helped raise Grelon. Raymond Pleasant, of Merriville, Indiana, gave a gift to his maternal grandfather, James Adams. Carlton Morris, of Merriville, Indiana, gave a gift to his maternal grandmother, Doretha Mosley Adams. Michael Morris, of Merriville, Indiana, gave a gift to their maternal great uncle, Dock Wade, who also was in Grelon's counsel of fathers. Troy Brodie, of Lithia Springs, Georgia, took his gift of Grelon back to "Granny," Lucinda Weston.

The "honorary" Posse male cousins, who loved Peanut and were raised with the rest by the Motherhood Counsel, are Ibn Pleasant, of Phoenix, Arizona; David Adams Jr., of Cleveland, Ohio; Ean Adams, of Miami, Florida; Tracy Adams, of Hammond, Indiana; Noah Adams, of Weidstrasse, Switzerland; Calvin Mosley, of Gary, Indiana; Thomas Mosley, of Gary, Indiana; Calvin Weston, of Gary, Indiana; Cab Weston, of Detroit, Michigan; as well as Johnny Mosley Jr. and Eddie Adams Jr., who preceded Grelon into eternity. Please pray for all of these young men and the families that they represent as Grelon Renard "Peanut" Everett was returned, ashes to ashes and dust to dust, until Jesus Christ cracks the sky and all of the dead in Christ are raised victorious. To God be all the glory for the life and the new life of a beloved gift from God, Grelon Renaurd Everett.

INTRODUCTION

No nursing home for me! I was not a responsible steward! Yet old age has crept up on me. I can no longer work, so I am checking into the Holiday Inn! With the average cost for a nursing home per day reaching $188, there is a better way when we get old and feeble. I have already checked on reservations at the Holiday Inn. With combined long-term stay discount and senior discount the cost is $49.23 per night. That leaves $138.77 a day for breakfast, lunch, and dinner in any restaurant I want and room service. Laundry, gratuities, and special TV movies are included. Plus, they provide a swimming pool, a workout room, a lounge, washer, and dryer. Most have free toothpaste and razors, and all have free shampoo and soap.

They treat you like a customer, not a patient. Five dollars worth of tips a day will have the entire staff scrambling to help you! There is a city bus stop out front, and seniors ride free. The handicap bus will also pick you up if you fake a decent limp. To meet other nice people, call a church bus on Sundays. For a change of scenery, take the airport shuttle bus and eat at one of the nice restaurants there.

While you are at the airport, fly somewhere. If you didn't act responsibly and save towards your golden years, don't worry. It takes months to get into decent nursing homes. Holiday Inn will take your reservation today. And you are not stuck in one place forever; you can move from Inn to Inn, or even from city to city. Want to see Hawaii? They have a Holiday Inn there too.

TV broken? Light bulbs need changing? Need a mattress replaced? No problem. They fix everything and apologize for the inconvenience. The Inn has a night security person and daily room service. The maid checks to see if you are okay. If not, they will call either the ambulance or the undertaker with no fuss. If you fall and break a hip, Medicare will pay for the hip, and Holiday Inn will upgrade you to a suite for the rest of your life. And there are no worries about visits from family; they will always be glad to find you, and probably check in for a few days' mini-vacation. The grandkids can use the pool. What more can you ask for? So, when I reach the golden age I'll face it with a grin. Just forward all my e-mails to: me@HolidayInn! (Anonymous, from the fabulous e-mail "library!")

> The pain of discipline is short, but the glory of its fruit is eternal. (Harriet Beecher Stowe)

PRAYER

Great God, giver of every good and perfect gift, we ask now for the power. Help us to look carefully at how we walk, not as unwise but as wise persons making the most of the time and the abundant resources that you provide us. The earth is yours and so are we. Teach us, afresh and anew, how to live as good managers and wise stewards of all that you entrust to our charge.

Gracious God, with the power, the authority, and the name of Jesus Christ, I come against any and every conflicting and confusing spirit that keeps us from offering unto you our very best. I bind every hindering spirit that your Word of faithful stewardship will go forth with clarity and with better understanding, reaping bountiful harvests in our lives.

Generous God, by your Holy Spirit, enable us each to better understand what your perfect will is for the stewardship of our lives. May we each be filled with your Spirit, rejoicing evermore with one another, in the harmony of song, praise, and thanksgiving for everything that is accomplished through the living of our days, in the name of our Savior, Jesus Christ. It is so.

1

GOD'S BOUNTIFUL BENEFITS PLAN!

The Begging Bowl

2 KINGS 8:1–6

There is no way to dress it up. There is no method of easing the distress. I don't care how many routes you travel to get there, applying for public welfare, public assistance, and even disability is humbling, embarrassing, and stressful. I had come to the place where I had to put in an application for help. This nonverbal message said, "I have come to the end of my rope." It said that my resources had been depleted, my ability to do for myself was cut off, and all the tricks up my short sleeves had been exhausted.

When I arrived at the place of public assistance, I stood before a hand-out system saying that I could no longer do what was necessary for myself. I needed help. I had arrived at the juncture where aid was required. It didn't matter how well I dressed, how much education I had attained, or how impressive was my resume of past academic achievements. It would not impress the individual who would receive my application for assistance.

My stance, in the front of a desk where provision to the needy was distributed, said that my economic well had dried up, my resource bank was depleted, and my means of self-support had run out. I was there to beg for help. There was no way to fix it up and make it pretty. There was no easing my feelings of distress. First and foremost, walking in the doors required an interior admission of helplessness. My asking for the application demanded submission to an ongoing, totally invasive process.

Filling out the multiple forms required providing information that I don't even talk to my mother about. The evidence required of me all sorts of organizational and administrative skill that I might not even have possessed. These kinds of inquiries can be demeaning. The waiting process is stress-producing as people look others over, trying to figure out their stories. The investigation is grueling. Begging for help is always shame producing. I had already come to realize and admit that I am insufficient on my own. The time now came when I had to beg for help.

To beg is to take low. To beg is to debase oneself. To beg is to humble oneself. To beg is to grovel for one's basic needs. It's not easy to beg. There is no nice way to beg. There is not much pleasure in the act of begging, asking, imploring, and beseeching. No one wants to beg. Americans don't like beggars. We are embarrassed by beggars. We are ashamed of beggars. Our ire is raised by beggars. Our indignation is expressed at beggars. For we want to be done with those who have to beg.

Let's bring this up close and personal. What's your first inclination when you see someone standing on a corner holding a bowl? Most of us will turn our heads and act as if we cannot see them. True? If they are standing directly in our path, holding out a bowl or a hat, how do you respond? If we can't get around them, we have to respond is some humane fashion.

Most of us, however, are not sure of how to provide what's necessary to a beggar. We ask ourselves, "What's appropriate?" "How much is enough to give?" "What will they do with my money?" "Am I simply enabling them?" "Am I being scammed?"

Most of the time, without even looking the individual in the eyes, without saying a kind word, without acknowledging that we really do want to be compassionate, we throw some loose change into the bowl and step away as quickly as possible. True? Come on, be honest. What thoughts come to your mind when you see a beggar in the distance?

Whatever negative images come to mind for you, they are probably also there when individuals come to your local congregation seeking mission assistance. Yes! Even at our pious, upstanding, do-good, faith-based ministries, we have poor attitudes when it comes to those who beg. We have a serious problem with folks who are not self-sufficient, independent tithers and givers.

As the federal government gives money to states and as faith-based projects begin to crop up more frequently, we, the church of the Living God, have to deal with our attitudes. The names have changed. The rules have been tinkered with so that "we" can control some of the money. We have to face the reality of "welfare reform" that speaks the language of faith-based partnerships and 501-C3s instead of the ministry of missions that we know so well.

The church has joined the secular world and said, "Let's change the way that we talk about 'those folks' who have come to ask us for help. Let's see if we can put a new political spin on it. Let's call it by another name and make ourselves feel more comfortable as we attend to their needs with our professional, well-dressed, cultured, and sophisticated selves!" We don't want to own it because it doesn't feel good and doesn't sound nice. In reality, however, the church is learning how to beg more effectively too!

Just watch the news as the Catholic Church tries to put a new spin on the handling of the millions of dollars paid out on account of pedophiles in the priesthood. It's affecting offerings. The Catholic

Church is trying various methods to generate more funds. This is called begging! And our annual, well planned and executed steward-ship campaigns are only refined methods of begging. So, how dare we have difficulty with "those" folks out there?

There is a biblical story that addresses "folks who beg." It's a story of a very wealthy woman who was kind to the prophet of God. She built him a room in her spacious home and offered him a place of respite, refreshment, and renewal as he traveled his circuit. They be-came great friends and had a mutual relationship. But a famine came upon the land. The prophet told the woman that she had to leave her vast holdings and go to a foreign land in order to survive.

For more than seven years, this unnamed woman and her family lived among strangers, as aliens, begging in order to survive. When the famine was over in her homeland, she and her child came home and entered into the court of the king. They came with begging bowls in their hands. She came to the king to beseech him for wel-fare. She came to the king seeking assistance, in order to be made whole. She came to the king with an appeal upon her lips for aid. She came into the presence of the king and said, "I ain't too proud to beg!" She was now a single mother with a child to care for.

Welfare and its entire gamut of sister reform acts are of direct concern to women and the children they bear. This story about a woman, her child, and her begging is close to me. For I have been on public welfare. I attended college, on welfare, with two sons to care for. I know the struggle. Been there. Done that. Don't need a t-shirt or cap. The experience is written upon my heart.

What I find amazing in the story is that it reads like this at its con-clusion: "So the king appointed an official for her . . ." This formerly wealthy, upstanding, and prominent woman was reduced to having a caseworker assigned to her. But the end of the story is the best. The king told the caseworker, "Restore all that was hers; together with all the revenue of the fields from the day that she left the land until now." This is not some recent and contemporary story, but a biblical story from the ancient text, found in 2 Kings 8:1–6.

So you can see that welfare is a biblical construct that was aimed at the restoration of an individual to a state of wholeness, soundness, health, and emotional well-being. We in America have a twisted concept of providing just enough for those in need to help them get by. As my Granny "usta" say, "They want us to get by on meager fare!"

There are two relatively recent publications in your local library. Both of them were released by Princeton University Press. Both of these books attempt to address the economic plight of America. Both of them seek to deal honestly, forthrightly, and candidly with this pressing issue of welfare reform. One book, *Work and Welfare*, is written by Robert Solow. Dr. Solow is a Nobel Prize–winning economist, who directs his attention to how we can get people off welfare and into self-sustaining jobs. Let's not talk about the reality that most "new" jobs pay minimum wage, don't provide medical or dental benefits, and don't allow folks to earn enough money to maintain their own apartments or participate in home ownership. Let's not address the reality that down-sizing, economic restructuring, and the economic spiral downward have all done their part to contribute to the increasing welfare needs of formerly well-employed, independent people.

Let's not deal with the truth that almost 90 percent of the wealth of the world is in the hands of about 3 percent of the populace. And most of the wealth in America can be directly traced back to foreparents who exploited, stole, and enslaved less fortunate folks in order to buy the boots and the shoelaces by which they have now "pulled themselves up." Despite not dealing with all of these truths, Dr. Solow has a ready audience for his book.

The other book, *It Takes a Nation: A New Agenda for Fighting Poverty*, is written from the research of Dr. Rebecca Blank. This is another look at how the "haves" can reduce the number of "have nots," who, with their begging bowls in hand, require too much of our hard-earned tax dollars and sheltered monetary gains. The issue, so academically addressed by both Dr. Solow and Dr. Blank, is a controversy that has even raised its ugly head in the church.

The question is being currently asked by good church goers, "Why should our local congregation provide 'welfare' for others who have the same opportunity to pull themselves up and get off their trifling backsides?" Go to the average church and you will find a food pantry or a clothes closet. And, if there is a food pantry, it usually serves once a week, while we eat three times a day and all the snacks included. Be sure to check what the good church folks have donated. You will find much "stuff" that neither they nor their children will eat. Don't forget to check out the clothes closet. There you will find junk that the Goodwill would not accept!

We in the church, have become Dr. "So-Low" and Dr. "Blank"! "Something must be done about those begging folks. We need funds for our new organ. We need funds for our spoiled, self-indulgent, and selfish youth. We need a Family Life Center for us." In God's church, there is little compassion for those who come with begging bowls in hand. Our low-down attitude makes us feel superior. Our minds have gone so blank that we actually have forgotten that each and every one of us is a beggar! We don't have a clue that each and every one of us on the planet earth is on public welfare! Yes! This includes you, too!

The breath we breathe is from the public welfare of our God. The energy that sustains our productivity and intelligence is directly from the public welfare of our God. The food we eat, the harvest we reap, the earth, its seeds and grains that reproduce, all come from the public welfare of our God. The clothes we wear, the houses we live in, the cars we drive, the church buildings we use, the money we make, the jobs we hold, the stingy portions we try to dole out so niggardly to those in need, all come to us by way of God's public welfare. Don't ever get so stuck on stupid, so arrogant and so ignorant that you forget that you too are a beggar with a bowl in your hands!

Let the public welfare of God's generous portion of air cease. Let the waves and electrodes in your brain cease. Let your arms or legs not respond to the transmitters in your brain. Let your tongue cleave to the top of your mouth. Then let's see who has the largest begging bowl.

We can only do whatever small measure of restoring others to wholeness we do with our mission projects and faith-based initiatives because God's welfare plan is working. We can offer our itsy-bitsy outreach to those less fortunate in our communities because the welfare program of a loving God is working. And it works because we have caseworkers assigned to our case.

Thank God for those angels, our caseworkers, named Goodness and Mercy. These two work overtime to ensure that our begging bowls remain full and that we are not on the other side of the desk, pulpit, or faith-based reception space. Thank God that there is an established cycle to the public welfare reform plan that God has set into motion. It works.

The plan says that God gives to us in our begging bowls. Jesus came to make sure that it was "abundant." Then, we are to work with what is put into our bowl and make every attempt to use the gifts and talents we have to increase it. Finally, we are to share from our bowls with others, remembering who filled our bowl in the first place. As we give from our begging bowls, God replenishes. This is called the law of sowing and reaping. God wills that restoration, wholeness, and health are our portion. "Beloved, I pray that all may go well with you that you may be in good health, just as it is well with your soul" (3 John 2).

My sisters, not one of us is too good to cooperate with God's bountiful plan for the benefit of all humanity. This is a marvelous invitation for us to help our local mission group or faith-based ministry to reevaluate how we're addressing the needs in our communities. We are dependent upon God and interdependent upon each other. Yes! Even those of us who dare to wear designer clothes, who have attained pompous titles, who have earned degrees, and who possess a posturing attitude are welfare recipients. I thank God that those caseworkers have been assigned to our case and we have received so many multiple benefits that others felt we didn't need or deserve!

There is no question. There is no debate. We cannot take a compromise position with all the benefits sitting in our begging bowls. We must willingly, cheerfully, and enthusiastically work with God to envision, strategize, and offer our begging bowls to others. It is the very least that we can do. Establishing faith-based partnerships, volunteering, networking, and being community for each other is the way God designed the world. Whatever we offer is simply our reasonable portion of service and gratitude to the Awesome Mystery whom we call God.

Public welfare is our God-given legacy. Passing it on is our gift to God in return. The day of accountability is at hand. Those who come to us for help have another caseworker assigned to their case. God has called me and you to be their caseworkers for help, restoration, and wholeness. It's God's truth!

Woman Wisdom speaks: "Those who oppress the poor insult their Maker, but those who are kind to the needy honor him" (Prov. 14:31).

2

GOD'S GAME OF HOLY HOKEY POKEY

Responsible, Personal Stewardship

MARK 12:41–43

The tall, thin, white man is standing outside in front of a huge, nice-looking brick home. He says to the audience, "I have a great family. We have a nice house with four bedrooms. We even belong to the country club." Next we see him at the wheels of a nice looking car. He says to the audience, "How do you like my car? It's new." Finally, we see him riding across his two-acre spread on a large tractor, cutting his lawn. He asks the audience, "How do I do it?" As he flips hamburgers in his backyard with his family awaiting their meal, the tall, thin, white man confesses, "I'm in debt up to my eyeballs. I can barely pay my finance charges. Won't somebody help me?"

Some of us can laugh at this Lending Tree.Com television commercial. For too many of us, it hits too close to home. Why? Because today's average family has more debts than prior generations. Twenty years ago people only spent two-thirds of their disposable income on debt. Today household debt—including credit cards, car loans, mortgages, and student loans—topped more than 100 percent of our disposable income. With the economic upswing of the 1990s we have spent the equity in our homes, we have played with our 401Ks, and the average one of us is carrying more than eight thousand dollars in credit card debt.[1]

As that tall, thin, white man confesses that he is up to his eyeballs in debt and can barely pay his finance charges, then we know that those of us in black America are in debt way over our heads. In these past two years, we have found ourselves the victims of massive layoffs, job restructuring and eliminating, plant closings, and decreases in the stock market that now have us scratching both our heads and our backsides. It's been a massive plot, plan and economic strategy to hook us on credit, and it's worked.

On a www.google.com search for the history of credit I discovered that this overwhelming credit concept began in New York in 1812 when Cowperthwaite and Sons began selling furniture on installment. In 1831, the first building and loan association fixed monthly mortgage payments as a way to home ownership. In 1910, Sears began offering revolving credit loans. Then in 1919, GMAC (General Motors Acceptance Program) was born, and by 1924 three out of four cars were sold on credit. In 1950, Diner's Club issued the first entertainment card, while in 1958, BankAmerica issued the BankAmericacard (which became Visa), and in 1966 the Western States Bankcard Association introduced Master Charge (later MasterCard).[2]

Not only have "they" allowed us to have credit cards, they send them to us unsolicited. "They" know that we are short on deferred gratification. "They" know that we like to keep up appearances. "They" know that each month, we will charge way more than we can pay off, so high interest rates have became a way of life. "They" know that we will rob Peter to pay Paul. And, "they" know that we are really suckers when Christmas, Mother's Day, and Easter comes. We buy too many gifts, clothes, and shoes! Now we're in debt way past our heads. Who can help us? I came to announce that there is a way out.

Disciplined and responsible stewardship is the way out of debt and the fears of possible job loss. Disciplined, responsible stewardship is our ability to responsibly handle the entirety of what God has given us to manage. Psalm 24:1a declares, "The earth is the Lord's and all that is in it!" We don't actually own anything. We are simply stewards or managers over what God has entrusted to our care. Half of the parables of Jesus concern money and possessions. They all illustrate lessons in a revolutionary way of life as disciples.

Stewardship is not just about money. Stewardship is a spiritual issue that tells God just how accountable we are with the whole of our lives. With debts way past our heads, we have said to God that we are rich in things, but poor in soul. And I have to confess that I used to brag about my being an addicted consumer who didn't need recovery! I enjoyed taking home the "things." Let me tell you that I can empathize with that tall, thin white man on the commercial!

At one time, I had three American Express cards; a Platinum Corporate card; a gold personal card; and a blue card that gave me a line of credit. I had a MasterCard and Visa, most major store charge cards, and I usually had people who picked me up for preaching engagements to take me to Dillard's, before they took me to the hotel. My credit rating was excellent. I enjoyed saying those magic words, "charge it!"

Now, let me hurry to say that I have been a tither since I was a child. And I was living the American dream with the house, the two cars, the time-share vacations, and the fabulous clothes. Our money was coming in so nicely that about five years ago I decided to increase my tithe to 15 percent. It's a good thing that I did. For, almost three years ago, I was released from my last white congregation with the charge of knowing so much about the Bible that I was beating up on them. The bishop placed me on incapacity leave. It's a nice term for being laid off, pink slipped, or downsized.

Friends, I was on a leave of absence. We don't have space for me to talk about trying to juggle all my multiple credit card bills. I murdered both Peter and Paul trying to keep my husband from ever finding out how much debt "we" had. But the day came when I had to confess. The day came when I had to acknowledge what I'd done. The day came when I realized that I had been a poor steward of God's resources! I was a wasteful steward and the day of reckoning caught up with me in the same way that it caught up with that tall, thin, white man and with many of you.

Do you remember that kid's game of hokey pokey? We had to put in what body part the teacher called for at the time. You put in your right arm and then your left arm. You put in your right foot and then the left one. Hokey pokey is a game to teach young children their body parts. We put our head in and finally the leader says, "Put your whole self in." And, the truth is that we're not a winner until we put our whole self in.

Many of us want to put in our head, our intellect, our opinions, our decisions, and our dreams. Know that I have offered God my wishes, my desires, and my plans! But simply offering our head, as wise and as educated as we are, is not enough to win with God.

Many of us like to put in our arms. We don't mind doing a bit of sweat equity, helping others with worthwhile volunteer efforts. That's all good, but just arms, as strong as they may be, are not enough to win with God.

Many of us want to put in our feet. We are willing to go, to do, and to be the best missionary abroad. We love the global emphasis of the gospel and we will lend our feet to mission projects both at home and abroad. But willing feet, as steady as they are, won't win God's game of hokey pokey.

God demands that our whole self be involved in disciplined stewardship. The passage for today comes in the context of a temple scribe of the Law quizzing Jesus about the greatest commandment. Jesus looks him in the eye and says, "The first is, 'Hear, O Israel: the Lord our God, the Lord is one; you shall love the Lord your God with all your heart, and with all your soul, and with all your mind, and with all of your strength'" (Mark 12:29).

Translated into English, Jesus is saying, we must love God with (our heart) the seat of our emotions, with (our soul) our will that dictates our decisions, with (our mind) the place of our thoughts, and with (all of our strength) our deeds and actions. This is our entire self. We can't hold back anything if we want to win eternity with God.

Then Jesus goes on to say, "You shall love your neighbor as yourself. There is no other commandment greater than these" (Mark 12:31). The scribe wanted to stroke Jesus with affirmation and responded, "You are right, Teacher . . . 'to love God with all the heart, all the understanding and with all the strength' and 'to love one's neighbor as oneself'—this is much more important than all whole burnt offerings and sacrifices" (Mark 12:32–33).

Jesus looked at this man who had given a legal response and told him, "Brother you are not far from the kingdom of God" (v. 34). For the scribe gave lip service to the truth, but his heart was not in it. For Jesus reads the motivations, as well as the thoughts that we have about God. And, although I was and continue to be a tither, I was not fully loving God with my whole heart, nor was I loving my neighbor as I loved myself.

I had been caught up in looking as if I had it all. What God demands from us as disciples is how do we give away our time, our energy, our commitment, and our money for the sake of the gospel. Spiritual formation and my sanity demanded that I begin to look for ways to eliminate my debts and allow my mind to be transformed. Jesus is watching both how we live and how we give. Jesus gave his life, his head, his feet, his arms, and his all so that we might have life and have it more abundantly. Swimming in debt, or trying to figure out how to juggle finance charges on credit cards, is not abundant life!

We know Jesus as a lover of people, a caller of people, a feeder of people, a healer of people, even a great conversationalist with people, but today, Jesus takes a seat in the temple and becomes a people watcher. He's waiting and he's watching to see who really loves God with their whole hearts and who is eligible to win God's game of hokey pokey.

So Jesus watches the wealthy, the proud, and the employed give their offerings. He really does pay attention to what they are wearing, their demeanor, and the motivations of their hearts. For remember that Jesus reads our intent as well as our actions. He sits and he watches the posture and the pride as the employed population parade around the temple to deposit their offerings in the treasury.

There were no temple ushers. There were no brass plates to be passed. There were no large kettles and woven baskets to be used for the collection. For God's instructions to Moses were to have the people to bring God an offering. To carry your own monetary gift was a sign of both thanksgiving and gratitude unto God for the opportunity of being God's manager over resources. So the offering parade was on and Jesus was seated, just watching.

The folks came. Some threw in many coins to impress the temple leadership. Some had their servants pour in large amounts so that the clanging would indicate their generosity. Some had guards surrounding them to symbolize their stature in the community. Jesus sat and watched as many gave. But Jesus knew that none of them, for all they had given, had really played God's game of holy hokey pokey!

Whenever Jesus sat, whenever any rabbi sat, it was a sign of preparing to teach some lesson of great significance. Jesus wanted the disciples of all times to learn from his watching experience. For there, in the midst of the crowd, in the middle of this hypocrisy, here came a poor woman. She was not just poor in the sense that she was thought to be an insignificant female. She was poverty stricken. She had no male relatives to look out for her. She didn't have a backup plan. She was down to her very last. She was at the avenue of "What will I do and how will I survive? And Jesus was watching.

Sister didn't have any food stamps to bail her out. She had no welfare subsidy plan to fall back on. She had no relief program to come to her rescue. The food pantry had not come into existence. This woman was down to her very last. All that she had left to her name were two meager coins.

Common sense says that she should have kept these two coins and tried to find several more in order to survive another day. If she had two coins, common sense says, give God one and save the other to buy something to eat. Being a woman of color, I believe that she could have made a mean meal with a small bird and a little grain.

But the scripture is clear. This poverty stricken woman un-wrapped her coins and put them both into the offering. She played God's game of holy hokey pokey and put her whole self in. It was clear that she loved God with her whole heart, her whole soul, her whole mind, and her full strength. And Jesus said, "Truly I tell you, this poor widow has put in more than all those who are contributing. For all of them have given out of their abundance; but she out of her poverty has put in everything that she had, all that she had to live on."

That tall, thin white man needs to be introduced to the concept of disciplined stewardship. For the promise is that when we dare to give God back a simple 10 percent of our time, our gifts, and our cash, God will open the windows of heaven and pour out blessings that we won't have room enough to receive. I know that it's the truth. For I have watched God work miracle after miracle for us in the past two years. Because I continue to tithe off the top of every check that I receive, I have been able to look at a bill and tell God, "You know that I don't have it and you have promised to pour me out blessings!"

Not too long ago, I had a six hundred dollar payment to be made on a line of credit. I had juggled every bill and every dime to the very last of my abilities. I had run out of schemes and maneuvers. The jig was up and my hand had been called. I patted the bill, whispered a prayer, and went to sleep. The next morning, I got up and went into my office to work. Around ten o'clock, my husband brought my mail to me. I noticed an envelope with the name of one of my girlfriends, Rev. Michelle Cobb, who lived out of town. We had not talked recently. When I opened the card, there was a check enclosed. Can you guess the amount on the check? It was exactly six hundred dollars! You might ask how and why was this possible. It was possible because I had made a conscious decision to play God's game of holy hokey pokey. I invite you to consider it too.

When we are down to nothing, we know that God is up to something. If I'd never met this economic crunch, I could not write this book. Furthermore, I could not give you several clues to eliminate your debt and become a more disciplined steward of God's resources.

First, repent of being a wasteful steward. Second, commit to tithing. You can tithe from your unemployment check, your disability check, or your welfare check. No one has to know but you and God. We all know that even utility companies demand their money! So how dare we rob God?

Third, call your creditors and be honest. Negotiate lower payments or make arrangements to only pay the interest in order to keep your good credit rating. Fourth, ask God to help you to change your attitude. God's transforming power is able to work in us and through us so that we can consider setting a realistic budget. Attempt to put aside five dollars a week into a savings account and stick to it. Truthfully, many of us don't have any savings to use on a rainy day.

Fifth, break those costly habits of eating out. If we ever calculated how much we spend each day at fast food places, we'd be shocked at how it adds up. Go to the store. Learn how to save money by buying in bulk and prepare some healthy, home-cooked meals. Pack a lunch. Make the kids pack a lunch. The savings will gladden your heart!

Sixth, bank your income tax refund next year! Bank the next "tax credit" check that is intended to "stimulate the economy!" It only makes the rich wealthier and the not-rich poorer! Seventh, covenant to not charge or buy expensive Christmas gifts. Give gifts made at home. Give homemade love. Make some jelly, some jam, or some cookies. Give a "gift certificate" with the services that you will provide during the next three months. Or set a date for a fun but inexpensive outing within the next thirty days.

Learn to value and give a gift of your time to spend with someone. Donate time at a shelter and take the children with you. The reality is that we are the gift to others! Finally, call the local Habitat For Humanity in your area and find out what nonprofit organization they refer clients to for "credit repair" workshops. There is government money available to help low- to moderate-income households repair credit, help pay off debts, and, if income qualified, even buy a home. They are able to assist with breaking leases on apartments and helping to fix damaged credit. Financial management, budget assistance, and economic literacy classes are provided free of charge within our local communities.

Sign up for a new class. Go! Learn some better stewardship principles and habits. Be led in a new and a different direction to become more socially responsible, fiscally wiser, and more disciplined in your stewardship responsibilities to God.

Jesus is watching you and me today. On Calvary, he gave us his all. In order to see his face in peace, we have to give our all too. God's game of holy hokey pokey demands that we put our whole selves into disciplined stewardship. Our hearts, our souls, our minds, and all of our strength are the essential parts of God's game. Alright, the game is on! Ready to play?

3

ADVENT, THE BREAKTHROUGH OF GRACE

Responsible Thanksgiving

LUKE 3:21–22

Iyanna, a two-year-old charmer, sat down on the kitchen floor at her grandmother Pastor Florida Morehead's home with her dinner placed before her on a tray.

The child folded her hands, closed her eyes, and, unbidden, said her grace. "God is great. God is good. Let us thank God for our food. By God's own hands, we all are fed, give us, Lord, our daily bread. Amen." The baby stopped to acknowledge her "daily bread" as a gift of grace from God.

A minister in training, Sista Janae, went to two Blockbuster Video stores to get me a film that I really wanted to see. I was so very grateful that she regarded my request as serious. She was kind and went out of her way for my sake. That Saturday evening Pastor Flo and I watched a fine movie. Janae was a great gift of grace to us.

I was at Shalom Ministries Christian Church, in Fort Washington, Maryland, with my girlfriend, Flo. She and her two daughters, Sonya and Erika, went out of their way to be gracious during my visit. The Women's Ministry had gone beyond the call of duty in order to ensure that my time with Shalom was blessed. The people at this church know how to make you feel special. If it were possible, I would have been passing out thousand-dollar gratuities for their helpful services. I will never forget the days that I spent in their presence and all the little grace notes that they added to my life.

Grace notes are those little additions played to spice up a simple melody. Grace notes are not essential to the original score. But they add so much to the music. In the black church, we find phat vamps, tight bridges, and repeated trills added as grace notes.

Even the secular world knows about amazing grace. They would never call it an act of God, but credit card companies, rental car agencies, and mortgage institutions extend to us, their customers, an undeserved and unasked for grace period to pay our bills. Some of the major magazines will send you a couple of months free, when your subscription expires. This is done, free of charge, or *gratis*, the Latin word for grace. This simple act encourages us to resubscribe.

On the flip side of all of these gracious deeds, I really dislike ungrateful people. When I do something for someone, go out of my way to be nice, especially if I have to spend additional money to purchase you a gift, if I don't receive a thank you note in short order, you will be labeled an ingrate. No more gifts will arrive from me, either!

God knows that my Mom raised me to send thank you cards early on in life. Born in Mississippi, I don't know where she learned this practice. But she surely enforced it in us. If one of my children fails to follow this acceptable method of courtesy, with one of my family members or friends, I'm embarrassed and will call them a family disgrace!

While I was in Maryland, a young black attorney was shot in the head, stabbed repeatedly, and then had his car pushed into a ravine in an attempt to drown him. Needless to say, the young man died. There seems to be very little saving grace to be extended to the individuals who killed him with such brutality.

Michael Jackson and I are from the same home town, Gary, Indiana. There used to be a time, when he was little and cute, that I felt proud of my "homie." Now that he has fallen from grace, in a very public and ugly way, I keep my mouth closed when the conversation rolls around to his name.

America has a way of officially stamping disapproval on any one who offends the government by an act of treason. We are sort of unforgiving. For the individual is labeled *persona non grata*, or person without grace. But America does not have the last word on who gets grace. The season of Advent gives notice to the whole world that the One who offers grace to "whosoever will come" and receive it has come, is present, and will come again!

In divine, loving mercy, the Sovereign God sent Grace into all of the world on that first Christmas night. John the Baptist went into all the regions around the Jordan crying, "Prepare for a breakthrough! Get ready for the arrival of Amazing Grace! Responsible stewardship is required." Read Luke 3:1–18 and get a real picture of John's message to the church of God.

In the year of the second wave of Bushes, when George, the Junior, had been "selected" to the White House; when Colin Powell, the son of Caribbean immigrants, was secretary of state; when Condoleezza Rice, an African American scholar, was national security advisor; when a black female, Carol Mosley Braun, and a black male, Rev. Al Sharpton, were both running for president of the United States; when a gay Episcopal priest had been elected to the episcopacy—it was a crucial time in America. It was a perilous time in the world. But it was due time that the Word of Grace was announced again to folks wandering in the wilderness, seeking a breakthrough.

Jesus was the Only Begotten Son of God. Jesus was born of a virgin, whose name was Mary. Jesus had angels sent to announce his arrival to the shepherds. Jesus had a bright star, twinkling and leading the Wise on a journey that took years. But, when Jesus put on flesh and stepped on the down escalator of time, reversed the power that had spoken life into the world, became an infant who needed a mother's womb to house him until the time for him to be expelled into human existence, Jesus needed a PR man to announce him to the world. John the Baptist was the right one, baby!

John the Baptist was known as a crazy kook! He looked strange. He dressed strangely. He ate a strange diet. He had no acquaintance with political correctness. But John had been the miracle baby of a priest, Zachariah, and an old, sanctified woman, Elizabeth. His reputation was that of a man who was in direct relationship with God. And God gave to this strange man the mission to get the church ready for the advent of grace into the world.

Grace is a free gift. Grace is an undeserved gift. Grace is something offered to us out of God's loving generosity. For God so loved the world that God gave Grace in the person of Jesus Christ.

We cannot command grace. We cannot dictate grace. We cannot legislate grace. We can only receive grace and be responsible for the gift. John says to us that in order to receive this free gift, we have to prepare. We must get ready. We must have our minds transformed. We are required to have our thinking changed. For with the free gift comes the price of responsible stewardship.

The Christian year allows us four weeks before Christmas to prepare our hearts to receive grace with readiness. Grace is not coming into a mess. Grace is not coming due to our superficiality. Grace is not coming into a manger that is not clean and prepared. Grace demands straight paths. Grace requires repentance for our continually missing the mark of God's standards of holy living. Grace must have a clean space in which to operate freely. Grace comes to take care of business for God.

When grace breaks through, valleys, low places, and depressed areas are lifted. When grace breaks through, high places, vanity-filled egos, and mountains of oppression must come down. When grace breaks through the crooked, the twisted, the diseased, and the afflicted will be straightened, healed, and made whole. When grace breaks through the rough places, the mean times and the seasons of desolation and despair are smoothed away. Grace comes to bring God's salvation.

Luke, the Evangelist, is also a physician, a healer, a shaman, and a doctor. Luke is concerned about the sick being made well. Luke wants the Gentile world to recognize that a perfect human being and a divine Deity was contained in the single person of Jesus. Luke wanted the world to know that Grace had broken through time so that we, sinful humanity, might be redeemed, rescued, transformed, and made fit stewards for all of eternity.

Luke shows us John giving a lecture on grace to the church. When the crowds began to seek John out for water baptism, the new "religious practice" in town, this crazy man exploded on them. "You brood of snakes! Why are you slithering down here to the river? Do you think that a little water on your snake skins, a little tenderizer on your rotting flesh, is going to deflect God's judgment? It's your life that must change, not just your snake skin!" In other words, John said, the change must come from inside. We cannot wear grace like an add-on coat.

Grace dwells inside a clean and a grateful heart. John wanted the people to know that a Savior from our sin was coming. He was going to slip in among them in God's way. This meant that the rituals of the Temple were no longer sufficient. John said that the church had to break away completely from sin. The normal and customary way of thinking and behaving had to be broken down interiorly.

Grace demands a breaking apart of evil associations, unsaved relationships, and all of our little idol gods. The power of God must be allowed to break into our opinions and our choices. Church folks have to break into their secret closets, break apart our day with prayer, with personal devotion, with scriptural meditation, and with sacred silence so that we might fully surrender and yield ourselves unto God, as good stewards.

Grace breaks in when we give up trying to do it our way. Breakthrough comes when we learn how to allow God to break down our stony hearts and to give us hearts of flesh that can receive this free gift. Breakthrough happens when we permit God to work in us with sanctifying power and with purifying fire. Advent announces that Christ is about to break into the whole of our lives. Breakthrough is not predictable as to when it will arrive. Breakthrough is not committed to what we have outlined to occur. Breakthrough is often old answers to ancient prayers that we, like John's father, the priest, have forgotten. Sometimes, the answers that God sends will look as strange as John and render us silent too! Breakthrough comes in unexpected times, unanticipated people, and unusual occurrences. Angels continue to show up, unannounced, into the sleeping spaces of clean people, both men and women!

One of the most unusual appearances of grace is found whenever we commune. We tend to forget that Jesus was born to die! We fail to remember that Jesus was the gift, slain before his birth. His mission was fixed. His determination was set. His mind was made up and his life was the atonement for the sin of the world. This is amazing grace, all by itself.

On the night that he was betrayed, Jesus played the role of a mother and cleansed the children before their meal. Responsible stewardship was at work. Then Jesus became the host of his own banquet and broke through the Jewish law to establish grace and truth. Jesus broke down all the barriers and allowed you and me to be welcomed at his table.

Jesus, who paid it all, invites us to come and to dine, free of charge. All that Jesus wants us to do is to be prepared to receive his grace with clean and thankful hearts. Thanks be to God for a season of preparing for the advent of amazing grace. I want to be ready. I want to be grateful.

In June 1990, the *Boston News* reported a story of amazing grace, combined with responsible stewardship. An engaged couple had gone to the Boston Harbor Hilton and made elaborate arrangements for a huge wedding, with reception and orchestra. They were required to pay a seven-thousand-dollar deposit.

A couple of months before the planned event, the young man decided that he needed more time before making this type of commitment. The engagement was called off. A distraught young woman went to the Hilton sales and catering office to cancel the date.

The sales manager was very gentle in listening to the story with empathy. However, a contract was involved. Very little cash could be returned. The woman who had been jilted decided to go ahead and use the seven thousand dollars to throw a big party on the same night. She had been homeless at one time in her life, and she remembered her defeated spirit while digging through garbage bins and having to eat at shelters. She decided who her guests would be at her "reception."

She sent invitations to the shelters in town. She mailed invitations to those places that ran a food pantry. She sent invitations to agencies that had workers with contacts on the streets. The only thing that she changed on her menu was to offer only "boneless breast of chicken" in honor of the man who had left her high and dry!

That night the rag tag and smelly—women with bags and women who had johns, those who didn't look quite right and those who were certainly overdressed—all came to the Hilton. They were greeted by smiling doormen. They were served by an elegant wait staff. They danced to the music of a live band. And they ate, free of charge, from a banquet table paid for by a woman they did not know.

Every diner experienced grace, unmerited and unheard-of favor, from one who could have been bitter, hard-hearted, and cruel. But she was a responsible steward over the resources that God had blessed her to have. I just pray that all the diners were grateful and on their way back into the cold night stopped and said, "Thanks!"

Responsible thanksgiving comes from a heart well attuned to grace. The Holy Meal to which we have been invited, free of charge, demands our gracious response. The Host invites us, the table is set, and the feast of God is open to whosoever will come. This is the best news of all!

4

DON'T BE NO FOOL!

Responsible Living

EPHESIANS 5:15–21

Once upon a time there was a tribal king in a village in Africa. There was trouble, confusion, and turmoil on every side. The king was always meeting with heads of state and other village officials making every attempt to keep peace among the warring neighbors. Because there was so much bad news, the village elders had employed a young man to entertain the king and to bring some light merriment into his life. The young man was soon called the village fool.

The young man became an expert in getting a laugh out of the old monarch. He was quite proficient in the art of "cutting the fool," as the elders said. The king became quite concerned about this young man's future. For you can only play the part of a fool for so long before it causes you great difficulty in your adult life. So the king ordered a wonderful walking stick to be fashioned from an old tree in the yard. And he called the young village fool and gave him a new assignment.

"Lad, I want you to take this walking stick and make visits into the other villages. Stay for awhile in each one and see if you can find someone out there who is a bigger fool than you. When you find them, give them this walking stick. Then you can return home."

The village fool began his trek across the land. He walked and he talked. He stayed with folks. He listened to other young men. But he didn't find anyone who was a bigger fool than he was. About six months into his trip, news reached him that the old king was dying, so the lad decided to return home. When he arrived, he asked to see the dying king to report his failure of the mission that had been assigned to him.

As he sat by the dying man's bedside, he asked the king, "Sir, can I ask you three questions?" The king nodded yes. First question: "Sir, have you ever done anything for anybody else that would not benefit you?" The dying king said, "No." Second question: "Sir, have you ever shown genuine love to anyone outside of your family? The dying king said, "No." Final question: "Sir, have you ever given thought to where you will spend eternity?" The dying king said, "No." "Well, Sir," said the village fool, "I'm going to give you this walking stick. It seems as if you deserve it."

It appears that the village fool was not as big a fool as the king and the king's cabinet had taken him for. The fool had wisdom enough to consider his life. The fool had wisdom enough to know that our world is larger and more inclusive than our immediate family. And the fool had enough wisdom to know that eternal life is based on our spreading the love of God around.

The Book of Ephesians is a plain text for our daily lives. The village fool's three questions to the dying king become a central issue for each one of us. Have we ever done things for others without regard for being repaid? Do we know the genuine, loving, and accepting love of God and do we share it freely with others? And, finally, do we know with assurance that our life will be spent in eternity with God?

Take a look at Ephesians 5:15–20. This text calls for each one of us to be discerning and discriminating regarding our walk with Christ. We cannot play the part of the village fool. We cannot spend our lives trying to make others laugh while the world is going to hell in a hurry. With fires raging out of control across the world, with other foreign nations threatening to blow us into extinction, with our national arrogance that has been thrown into our face time after time while we declared war and yet have not caught or killed Osama Bin Laden, the declared mastermind of the World Trade Center destruction on September 11, 2001—it's time for the church to be on a straight course with holy living.

The world situation is bad, and the national economy is getting worse. Jobs are being pulled, closed, transferred, and wiped out by computers. The time has come that we must face the reality that God alone is our source. Regardless of what we know, who we know, or how long we have known this person or that one, nothing is steadfast and dependable but our relationship with God.

Therefore, it requires prudence, deliberate effort, thoughtful choices, and wisdom to know and to live the will of God. Slip-shod, politically correct, worldly living will evidence that we are "unwise" people who deserve the walking stick from the village fool.

My mother and my grandmother used to warn me repeatedly, "Gal, don't you be no fool!" Yet I have made some very unwise choices in my life. If the truth be known, all of us have played the part of the fool at one time or another. It's a human element. It's a human trait. It's a human fact that we will make some bad choices. We need disciplined and responsible stewardship to become a regular part of our lives.

So Paul is writing to church folks and saying that, with our new birth experience, we have some different options to consider. We have some alternative experiences that we can select. We have a different route on which we are to journey if we want to be called wise. Verse

15 says, "Be very careful then how you live, not as unwise people but as wise, making the most of the time, because the days are evil."

Paul goes into detail about our bad choices because the days in which we live are evil. It's a hard reality that the devil is running rampant in the world. Enron, the Arthur Anderson Company, Martha Stewart, and WorldCom have made it plain that people in the world continue to steal and feel that they can get away with it.

Paul says to you and to me in Ephesians 4:27–28: "Do not make room for the devil. Thieves must give up stealing; rather let them labor and work honestly with their own hands, so as to have something to share with the needy." Don't be no fool and feel that the slick and manipulative ways by which we used to make a living will carry us into eternal life. It's about old-fashioned work that we are now called.

It's about discovering and knowing your gift area so that it can make a living for you. It's about being effective in the body (the church) where God has called us and knowing that the eye of God is always seeking those who need favor. It's a promise from 2 Chronicles 16:9 that, "The eyes of God range throughout the earth to strengthen those whose hearts are true."

Wisdom demands that we seek to develop a set of spiritual senses that result from our transformed minds, our purposeful study, and our continual in-filling of the Holy Spirit. God is not calling us to be deep and mystical. God is not telling us that we ought to resort to following so-called prophets for a word or be addicted to fortune tellers or our horoscope in order to know God's will. This is a simple prayer request: Spirit of the living God, fall afresh on me. Spirit of the living God, fall afresh on me. Melt me. Make me. Fill me. Use me. Spirit of the living God, fall afresh on me."[1]

Tongue speaking and interpretation are not required. Prophetic utterance and being slain in the spirit are not mandated. Running the aisles and knocking over pews won't attain wisdom any faster. But simply praying, asking and receiving the gift of the Holy Spirit provides new life for these evil days. This is why Paul says, in Ephesians 5:18, "Do not get drunk with wine," reefer, coke or any of those other substances that will lead us quickly downhill to sexual promiscuity, filthy practices, and bullying greed. Rather, we are to be filled with God's Spirit, who teaches us the wisdom of Jesus Christ, who is the Living Word and the role-modeling will of God.

The words of Paul, urging us in the book of Ephesians to walk as those who are wise, refers the church back to the life of the wisest man who ever lived, King Solomon. The Old Testament reading is a summary of the reign of David's and Bathsheba's son. The story reminds me a lot of my friend, the Rev. Dr. Eleanor L. Miller, who took over the "reign" after the death of her father, Rev. Eddie Miller. She is currently the senior pastor of Sureway Missionary Baptist Church in Chicago, Illinois.

This passage speaks about the succession to the throne of one who had no military victories, nor any great and popular aggregation of the tribes seeking his kingship. Solomon gets the throne because God made a covenant with his father. The Bible records that "God loved him (Solomon)" (2 Sam. 12:24).

In other words, Solomon is the first genuinely dynastic accession to the throne because God put him there. There was no popular seeking of a king as with Saul. There was no takeover of the throne as both Annon and Absalom, Solomon's older brothers, had attempted. Rather, God's hand was upon Solomon due to the wisdom that he exhibited.

I have many female friends who are pastors; I have many male friends who are pastors. Of them all, I consider Eleanor Miller to be the wisest, most responsibly disciplined steward that I know. God loved Eddie Miller for his wisdom and his love for the sure way of God. And God loves Eleanor Miller for the very same reason and placed her on this earth to continue the dynasty of her father.

If you read the books of Deuteronomy, Joshua, Judges, Samuel's collection, or both chronicles of Kings, you will find that they all seek to explain the disaster of the exile of Israel from the promised land. In their examination, they discover that with very few exceptions, they had been enslaved, not due to negligence on God's part, but due to the sin of the people, who chose not to walk in wisdom. They had a history of sin. They refused to obey the statutes, the commandments, and the ordinances. They would not listen to the priests, the prophets or the kings. By God's standards, all of the kings, including David, had fallen short.

But God's covenant with David stood. According to the history, only Solomon, Hezekiah, and Josiah were wise and faithful kings. All the rest were judged and found lacking. Responsible stewardship in daily living does not come "naturally." It demands prayer, practice, and more prayer and practice in order to cultivate it as a habit in our lives. Solomon was a young man when David died. God came to inquire, "What do you want from me?" (1 Kings 3:5). Of all the things that a young man could have sought and been given, Solomon acknowledged that God had been faithful to his father, David. Then he faced up to the fact that becoming the pastor, leader, and judge of God's people was a difficult task and that he had little to bring to the table. So the most important thing that Solomon recognized was that he needed wisdom to have the capacity for judicious and discerning leadership abilities.

I've spent time much with Eleanor, and even in the late watches of the midnight, she's waiting and listening for the wisdom and the sure way of God. She does not give fast and glib answers. She is not known as one of the village fools. She is a sage, a counselor, a great woman, mighty in handling the living Word, and one who will call you on a fast quickly. For like Solomon, she recognizes that without God, she is nothing, without God she would have already failed. For time is filled with swift transitions and church pews are filled with folks who have itching ears. So Eleanor's prayer has been and continues to be "I want to live so that God can use me, anytime and anywhere." Like Solomon, she waits on God for wisdom.

"God grant me wisdom, so that I might know how to govern this great people and to distinguish between right and wrong. For who is able to govern this great people of yours?" (1 Kings 3:9). Solomon gave the right response. All of the doors to God's resources swung open for him. Because the lad did not ask for riches or a long and fruitful life, he got those too. The Bible says, "Seek ye first the kingdom of God and all these other things will be added to you." (Matt. 6:33).

Eleanor did not have her father's maleness. She did not have his girth and his booming voice. She did not have his male connections. And she did not have the popular appeal of the Chicago church world. But, like Solomon, she had her father's God. This makes all the difference in the world.

The tradition of the legends of Solomon's wise rule is set forth in this passage. The royal messianic picture is painted in which Jesus will come to establish justice and righteousness and to provide the proper political structure for the people of God. For the king, and by definition, the pastor and all political leaders, are God's servants for the people.

God is pleased to grant wisdom to all of us who will ask. The emphasis on wise living, wise decisions, and wise judgments tells us about the benchmarks of those who stay in close relationship with wisdom's source.

There was a transition of power when Solomon asked God for wisdom. His wise leadership was evidenced among his people. Solomon was a true worshipper. The whole setting is one of a liturgical event where the king went to sacrifice at Gibeon. The Temple had not been built, for the blood on David's hand couldn't touch it. But Solomon was selected, authorized, and appointed by God to build the Temple because his heart belonged to the Sovereign.

Eleanor Miller practices, like Solomon, the responsible stewardship disciplines of holy living, worship, prayer, meditation, listening, and scripture reading. She keeps a song on her heart. She practices living a life of thanksgiving. She role models Christ at work among the people. For wisdom is not about education, degrees, or even common sense. Wisdom is about being so aligned with God that even our lack of information will not lead us to destruction.

Let me measure my friend Rev. Dr. Eleanor L. Miller by the three questions of the village fool: 1) Has she ever done anything for someone without any thought of being repaid? She's done so much just for me, I just can't tell it all! 2) Does she show the accepting, affirming, and challenging love of God at all times? She has loved me unconditionally . . . and that takes a lot! 3) Does she live a life that makes me sure that she will live with God throughout eternity? I'd bet my last dime on her being there!

Well, it's a sure thing that she will not receive the fool's walking stick. But, how about you and me?

Paul says it like this, for our consideration: "Be very careful then how you live, not as unwise people but as wise, making the most of the time, because the days are evil. So do not be foolish, but understand what the will of God is . . . be filled with the Spirit" (Eph. 5:15–18). Don't be no fool . . . there is a definite need for our practice of responsible stewardship.

5

THE CHURCH, GOD'S ACCEPTABLE SERVANT

Stewardship for Community

2 SAMUEL 21:1–14

There is no need for an introduction or formal protocol. The agenda has already been established. There is no need to give an elaborate explanation of the theme for this book. For all of us are called to be living witnesses and personal testimonies that tithing, giving, and responsible stewardship is the role of every acceptable servant of the Most High God. We are to give as we have been blessed. We are to be cheerful givers. For we are the recipients of amazing and abundant grace preserved for us over the years.

During the years since the resurrection, Jesus Christ has left human beings as the keepers of the dream and the glue that holds communities together. For all of these years the church has moved into uncharted territories and persuaded others to follow its people to new heights in God. The church is as tall as a forest pine tree, which will bend as low as a weeping willow for the purposes of calling others unto

God with their struggles. People are invited to come unto God, just as they are, without resources, and to begin living from God's joyous plan of welfare. When I think of God's welfare plan for the church, I am reminded that, as a clergywoman, I know too much of the behind-the-scenes stories that have never been and will never be told.

However, there are more than enough stories of responsible stewards, gifted with the gift of giving, who need to be heralded for their contributions. The Bible provides us with many stories and our own personal journeys offer more besides.

We all know that these have been centuries of the church gathering people, pushing them to grow, to stretch their boundaries, reaching for those who are sinking, challenging systems to be more just, overturning obstacles that dared get in the way, linking hands with others who want to accomplish their divine purpose and depending upon the generosity of responsible stewards across the world, for there is no charge to come to Jesus Christ!

The church will link hands and join hearts with anyone who will pray and will support and push others to become their very best. We need to celebrate the church because of the multiple exploits, accomplishments, and endeavors that have kept congregations moving forward despite the changing political tides. We need to pause and to rejoice in the memory of the church's labors, to honor its various ministries, and to recommit to being more responsible as stewards ourselves.

There ought to be major music serenading the church with song. There ought to be bands, choirs, and orchestras playing the church a simple melody of love. There ought to be live flowers blooming, fragrant with scent to detail the touch that the church leaves wherever it has been established. The newspaper presses should be rolling. The television cameras should be rolling, recording, and registering our festivity. There ought to be whistle blowing, loud rejoicing, and merry dancing in the streets. We are part of a great cloud of witnesses because of the church of God.

The passage that allows me to view the church in all of its beauty comes from 2 Samuel 21:1–14. It is the story of Sista Rizpah, one of God's acceptable servants who practiced responsible stewardship on behalf of the whole community. For we do not "join" the church for just our family and ourselves! The church makes us family with folks all across the world and we are all responsible for one another.

This story is about a woman who was the intercessor for her entire community. This story is about a woman who made a decision and stuck to it, although she paid a heavy price. This story is about a woman who through loss, death, grief, and pain held out hope for God to send her a harvest of blessings. This is a story about a woman who didn't know what the outcome of her stand would bring, but she had a heart of faith. This is a story of a woman who became a valuable member of the God Squad and brought about positive and powerful change in the environment that she affected.

There had been a three-year famine in the land. Saul had committed a serious offense against the Gibeonites. It was an act that made him guilty of their blood. It was such an awful sin that God stopped the rain. Famine came and lasted for three years.

We know about famine. It's when the economy begins to slow down and jobs become scarce. We know about famine. It's when pink slips are given and unemployment benefits run out. We know about famine. It's when bills are high and income is low. Famine had come and lasted for three years.

For three years there had been no rain. The Israelites were farmers, and farmers needed rain for the crops. When the rain ceased, insects took over. When the rains stopped, there were no irrigation sprinklers, no underground water systems, no fertilizers, and no pesticides to prevent a famine. When God withheld the rains, the whole agricultural framework broke down.

There was a drastic food shortage in the land and King David went to inquire of God.

God told David "It's on account of Saul and his blood-stained house" (v. 1). When David went to ask the Gibeonites what would make them happy so that God would release the rains, they wanted all of Saul's male descendants to be given them to be killed and to be exposed on a hill before the Lord (v. 6). David spared the life of Mephibosheth, the lame son of Jonathan but gave up the two sons of Rizpah and the five sons of Merab, Saul's daughter (v. 8–9). They were all put to death during the first days of the harvest, just as the barley harvest was beginning (v. 9).

Barley harvest began in late April or early May. The Bible declares that Rizbah went up on the hill and guarded the bodies of these seven dead sons of Saul. She stayed there, up on a hill with the dead and decaying bones of seven men, from the beginning of the barley harvest until the rain poured down from heaven. From April until October, the entire harvest season, Rizbah stood, all alone. From April until October, in the midst of a famine, God's acceptable servant guarded the bones that were hanging under an unrelenting sun.

There's a stench attached to death, but Rizbah stood her ground. Wild beasts tried to come and have a feast, but Rizbah stood her ground. The sun continued to come up with its heat, and the moon with the silence of death and aloneness, but Rizbah stood her ground. What do you do, when you've done all you can, and what you've done is never enough? What do you do, when your friends walk away, and there's no one around that you can trust? Crying didn't stop her standing. Wailing didn't stop her standing. Hurt didn't stop her standing. Grief didn't stop her standing. Decay didn't stop her standing. For almost six months, half of a year, this woman stood, alone on a hill. Where were her girlfriends? Where were her supporters? Where were her "road dawgs"? What did she eat? How did she cleanse herself? When could she sleep? What did she do about changing her clothes? Where was the other mother? Where were the grandmothers? We get no answers to these questions. What the text says, though, is that this acceptable woman of God stood through one of the most horrible situations that we could ever imagine until God answered prayers for the entire community.

Rizbah stood for the people of God. That's dead body number one. Rizbah stood for the sin of Saul. That's dead body number two. Rizbah stood for her own family. That's dead body number three. Rizbah stood for the sake of every male child. That's dead body number four. Rizbah stood for the sake of every crying mother. That's dead body number five. Rizbah stood for the sake of the king. That's dead body number six. And Rizbah stood as a prayer, a living testimony. That's dead body number seven.

Rizbah stood to show us a biblical picture of a contemporary woman. Rizbah stood to give us a role model of a woman who stands on behalf of the poor, the least, the forgotten, and the neglected. Rizbah stood to intercede for sinners. Rizbah stood for local community as a beacon of light. Rizbah had no respect of persons and represented both men and women, available to whomever.

But, finally, Rizbah stood for the sake of the King of Glory. For the church is a place of prayer, committed to the ministering work of Jesus Christ. He stood alone as they took him from judgment hall to judgment hall. He stood alone as they nailed him to an old rugged cross. He was laid alone in a borrowed tomb. He got up alone on Easter morning. But when he comes again, there will be a harvest gathering with him. For God has not only promised rain, but there is coming the latter rain! Why? The latter rains will fall because God honors the petitions of acceptable servants committed to responsible stewardship.

The bride of Christ is a woman of integrity. The bride of Christ is a woman who dares to stand alone. The bride of Christ is a woman who welcomes "whosoever will" to come, to enter, to join and to become a living part of the body ministry. The good news is that the whole world community benefits from the rains that are coming due to our responsible stewardship. The famine among us will end. The promised harvest of God will come. For the church of the Living God remains an acceptable servant of God who continues to stand strong due to those who are involved in various acts of responsible stewardship. And this is mighty good news.

6

A DANGEROUS LOVE

The Stewardship of Scarce Resources

RUTH 1:1–18

The words sort of hung there, in the air. They came with force, with passion, and with a serious conviction. The words were unforgettable. The words pierced the haunting silence. They cut across the chasms of fear, pain, regret, and grief. The words were unforgettable. The words cut to the very heart of the matter. They came with a resolve, with no regret, and without any hesitation. The words were unforgettable.

You know unforgettable. It's what's lasting, what's impacting, and what either adds or takes meaning away from your life. You know unforgettable. It's what's significant, what's life altering, and a powerful measure of time. You know unforgettable. Its' what's emotional, what's affective, and some matter that is psychologically piercing to your heart.

The words sort of hung in the air. They came with a lack of energy, a sense of emptiness, and without any hope. The words were unforgettable. Standing at the crossroads, with a life-changing decision already made, Naomi, a Hebrew woman from Bethlehem, said to her daughters-in-law, "Life has been very bitter for me. Life has been worst for me than for you, two strangers to the covenant, because the hand of God has turned against me" (Ruth 1:13).

The words hung there, in the air. "The hand of God has turned against me" signifies that this individual has been and is facing a period of desolation. "The hand of God has turned against me" tells me that we have a woman who is and has been filled with despair. "The hand of God has turned against me" declares to me that depression was active in Ruth, who symbolized and was a precursor to, the church of the Living God.

We don't want to deal with depression in the church. We want to believe that if we live right, if we sing it correctly, and if we can just get the riffs, the vamps, and the funky chords together, that depression will pick up and leave us alone. It's a lie. For depression is one of the satanic tools used to discourage the creative people of God. Depression is alive and well whenever we come to the end of a high time of celebrating, networking, teaching, learning, sharing, posturing, and profiling. My friends, we forever return to the crossroads. And whenever we reach them, like Naomi, it's another time for each of us to make a fresh decision.

Depression is not just a case of the blues. Depression is not just about simple and uncomplicated grief. Depression is not something that is lodged within the Caucasian race alone. Depression is not normal. Yet, depression is a sadness that will not go away. Depression is not just a mind game that we can pooh-hooch away. Depression is a mental condition that says, "I'm not worthy and what I do is not worthwhile. Depression is an interior emptiness that nothing seems to fill.

Depression will take us to a place where we may be susceptible to illicit sex, alcohol, drugs, and gambling. Depression will move us out of relationship with God and on a journey that we never thought that we would ever take. Without Godly wisdom and counsel, without prayer and, often, medical assistance we will find ourselves on a downward slope with no end in sight.

In Psalm 42, David describes depression as being in a "horrible pit." We get depressed when we really believe that "the hand of God has turned against" us. Naomi was standing at a crossroads. Naomi was depressed. It was time for a fresh decision.

The book of Ruth is only one of two books named after females in the Christian canon of scriptures. The book of Ruth seems like a simple tale of three women in Moab who happen to run into a series of bad luck. The book of Ruth appears to be a story of life gone sour for three widows. But, honestly, the story is about a dangerous love affair. The book of Ruth represents our complex social issues as Africans in America. It details the gender issues of the poor and the uprooted and of cross-cultural relations. The problem of interethnic marriage and holding onto God during difficult times all come to bear in the book of Ruth. It's here that we discover a dangerous love requiring firm stewardship of meager resources.

Born in Bethlehem, the "land of bread," Naomi and her spouse, Elimelech, and their two sons had moved from Bethlehem when a famine had come upon the land. They became strangers in a foreign town in Moab. In Moab, they were the outsiders. In Moab, they were the heathens. In Moab, how were they to sing the songs of Zion? In Moab, how were they to keep the kosher laws? In Moab, how were these sons and daughter of Judah going to extend the realm of the Most High God?

The Hebrew laws dictated that those desiring an office within their territory had to have claim and proof to Hebrew blood for two generations. But Moab was known as a place of sexual deviance, casual sex and promiscuity. Therefore, Hebrew laws claimed that no one from Moab would ever become a leader, for it required ten generations for their bloodlines to be cleansed. Talk about ethnic purity.

Talk about ethnic pride. Talk about snobbery, the Hebrews had it. But now four Hebrews were living in Moab.

Being agricultural people, every family needed children and wanted male children, to work the land. So the two sons of Elimelech and Naomi were forced to marry two women from Moab. Ruth and Orpah entered into a dangerous love affair with these foreigners. Life seemed to be settling down. But, as with you and with me, Mother Nature does not always play fair. Elimelech died, and soon after, both of the sons died. There were no offspring. Three women were left without the salvation of any man being present in their lives.

There were no welfare programs. There were no state subsidies. There were no provisions for widows or for strangers in a foreign land. And, to make bad matters worse, famine had come to Moab. These three widowed women were up a creek without a paddle. It felt as if Naomi's God, Jehovah-Jirah, had let her down. It felt as if Naomi's God, Jehovah-Nissi, had not come through. It surely felt as if Naomi's God, Jehovah-Shalom, had not provided her with peace. Practicing stewardship in a strange land had become a dangerous love affair for Naomi. She had been in love with and faithful to a God who did not come through for her. Naomi felt abandoned. Naomi felt forsaken. Naomi felt forgotten. As a matter of fact, Naomi was severely depressed. So, she decided that the best thing for her to do was to give up and return to Behtlehem and die among her people.

Death seemed like a sweet escape to Naomi and to many of us. Hopeless was all that Naomi felt as she packed up what she could carry in order to return "home" as an empty and lonely woman. She was in the midst of community at the crossroads. With her stood both Ruth and Orpah. But she was so far down, she had decided that relationships no longer mattered. "Life is filled with swift transitions," said a songwriter. And many of us have had one swift transition too many. Like Naomi, what will we face, beyond the crossroads? Like Naomi, there's been a famine at home! Like Naomi, our bread has run out and the emptiness is all that fills us. What will we do if we turn around and go backwards?

This fresh word is not about the music that we enjoy on Sunday morning. This fresh word is about the musicians, the choir members, the ushers, the lay folks, and the pastors who have been faking worship for far too long. This word is not about the roles that we play in worship, but this word is about our authentic relationship with a dangerous love! There can be no more "business as usual," for the crumbs that we have tried to live on have dried up! Oh, yes! We can learn a few new musical pieces. Folks, it's only crumbs. We can continue to rub elbows, make new connections, network, and trade e-mail addresses and fax and telephone numbers. But it's only crumbs. We will each stand at the crossroad, with Naomi. We will have to face the music of recalcitrant choir members, noncooperative pastors, and a listless "Let me see you entertain me" congregation. Beloved, we cannot survive off crumbs. The Giver of the Song demands an accounting of our relationship. It's time for us to make a fresh decision.

Will you please, repeat after me: THERE IS NO SPOT THAT GOD IS NOT! Say it again. Say it one more time. It makes no difference how depressed we might be. It makes God no never mind how low we have sunk into our pits. God could care less about what we have done in our past. God is waiting to see what it is that we want to do with this dangerous love affair that is being offered again. We're all at the crossroads.

It's a dangerous love, for you have got to make up your mind to follow the Bread. The bread had run out in Moab. Wherever you and I have been going, attempting to substitute our roles for an authentic relationship with God, has not fed us very well. We might have come to this day empty and alone, but we don't have to leave the same way.

When Naomi gave her daughters-in-law a wonderful benediction and tried to dismiss both of them out of her life, Orpah kissed her and walked off the scene of history. But, there is no spot where

God is not, and Ruth became the Christ figure in Naomi's life story. When we are down to nothing, God is up to something far exceeding what we can think, imagine, or ever conceive. When we have felt that God had forsaken us and forgotten us, God was writing a more grand design for our lives. When we felt that it was God who had failed, it was only our teaspoon of faith that really failed. For God said to Naomi, through Sista Ruth: "Do not press me to leave you or to turn back from following you! Where you go, I will go; where you lodge, I will lodge; your people shall be my people, and your God my God. Where you die, I will die—there will I be buried. May the Lord do thus and so to me, and more as well, if even death parts me from you!" (Ruth 1:16–17).

This is a dangerous type of love, my friends. For this love will not leave you. This love will not forsake you. You may walk away, but this Love is relentless. This Love is persistent. And this Love does not just want to leave the crossroads with you but longs to live within your very being and feed you, until you want no more. Naomi got the message. Naomi discovered that a crossroads could provide a step toward new possibilities of Fresh Bread. Ruth, the Moabite, turned and said to a depressed Naomi, "Let's go, Mother. I can smell the baking of the Bread."

Not only had God allowed Naomi to go through a difficult period and to encounter depression. But God had plotted and planned to bring her into the Jesus story, along with this cursed woman from a strange land. What a dangerous love. For a Moabite became the Grandmother of David, the king. And through her bloodline came Jesus, the Christ.

It's decision time at the crossroads. The Bread of Heaven longs to fill us until we want no more. The Bread is already prepared. The question is: Will we commit to following the Bread of Life through faithful stewardship that calls us to suffer and to wait? There are too many hungry people in the world. There are yet too many of us who need to make a commitment to Jesus Christ and to have a relationship with Fresh Bread. If you are tired of living off crumbs, just say, "I want Fresh Bread."

There are depressed folks in the church. There are those who have been down in the pit for so long, it seemed as if it was a normal place to dwell. If you are one who would like to come up out of that pit of depression, if you are willing to ask the Bread of Life to feed you and to point you in the right direction for godly counsel and mental health, just say, "I need some Healing Bread."

Perhaps you are one who knows that it's time for you to make a step in a different direction. You already know Christ in the pardon of your sin. You are fortunate and don't have an issue with depression. But you know that God is calling you to move from the crossroads and begin a new and different journey to Fresh Bread. Just say, "I will recommit to seeking daily and hourly guidance and direction from the Holy Spirit."

There is room at the cross for all of us. And, there is Bread enough for all of us. For in God there is no scarcity at all!

7

CAN WE FEED THEM ALL?

The Stewardship of Feeding the Hungry

JOHN 6:1–14

What's your take on the subject of local congregations and food pantries? Come on now, it is time to talk about this horrible subject.

How long is your pantry open each week? Is there any meat in the packages that you give away? How are people treated as they come to be "helped" by the "loving" members of your local congregation?

Are the members who "serve" filled with the love of God? Is there really a genuine spirit of hospitality at work among them or are they simply doing mission work without a sense of ministry?

If, God forbid, you and your family ever had to be the recipients of the food pantry, would you be willing to enter the local food pantry where you belong? The church does not have a loving history of ministering to the hungry among us.

In our gospel passage in the book of John, there was a huge crowd gathered around Jesus. They had all gathered for his dynamic, life-changing teaching, his awesome ministry of healing, and the power of the miracles that he works. Whatever their personal reasons for coming, the people had showed up in great numbers.

In Matthew 14:21, we find these words, which the evangelist John does not include: "And those who ate were about five thousand men, besides women and children." Now, at the foot of the cross, according to John 19:25, we find that there were three women and one man. That is almost the identical ratio of women to men in the church today. And, thankfully, we have lots of children due to the baby-busters! So, if the record shows that five thousand were fed, not counting women and children, we can with fair accuracy say that this vast crowd that was fed numbered well over fifteen thousand people.

So, in John 6:5, Jesus looks at the multitude and asked Brother Philip: "How are we to buy bread so that these people may eat?" In other words, what are we to do about the welfare of all these hungry folks?

"This Jesus said to test Philip. For Jesus already knew what he was going to do" (v. 6). When we look at all the needs of all the people around us; when we see the scarcity of our limited resources and know the vast and overwhelming needs of those who come to seek our help, our mission dollars, our "feel good" charity deeds, and our concern for their plight, the Jesus question is put before us again: "Can we feed them all? " It's here that we hedge, we punt, we begin to both add and subtract.

We in the church are quick to divide but seldom do we dare to multiply. Yet this is the challenge before us. In our individual life, in our corporate life as church gathered, can we feed, clothe, and nurture all the hungry souls who come our way? For this is our reasonable stewardship.

In verse 7, Philip provides a politically correct response. He begins to talk about the scarcity of resources: "We couldn't feed them all if we wanted to . . . we can never feed this crowd." There is not enough bread, not enough supplies, not enough allocated, not enough budgeted, and not enough considered to meet all of their needs. We would love to do it, but it's obvious that we don't have enough! Surely, you can see the size of the crowd and you already know that we would if we could, but we simply don't have enough!

Have you ever noticed that Jesus always took the simple things of life to explain the grand, magnificent, glorious, and beneficent realm of God? To use the metaphor of bread and wine to talk about the resurrection of his body and the blood shed for our salvation is deep stuff.

However, everybody is familiar with bread. For we all must eat. So Jesus, the Bread of Life, begins with what we all need in order to show the disciples and us a different way of meeting our needs. Jesus begins to show us his plan of feeding the hungry with responsible stewardship with a simple action. The main character in this welfare activity was not one of the adult disciples, but a little boy who willingly shared what his mom had prepared for him alone.

This particular story illustrates that the welfare of all the people was the primary ministry of Jesus Christ. Jesus says clearly and distinctly in Matthew 9:12, "those who are well don't need the physician, but I have come to minister to the sick." Then, his brother, the bishop of the church, summarizes his ministry in 3 John 1:2 as he records, "Beloved, I wish above all things that you would prosper and be in health, even as your soul prospers." Taking care of our sin business was the first priority of Jesus. However, he also met physical needs!

Jesus and the church that he founded was always concerned with the total welfare of the people. This story about feeding all of the multitude shows up in all four of the Gospels. However, John provides us with evidence that Jesus is using this time and place as a teaching tool for those with limited vision. We have heard Philip's politically correct response that didn't fly with Jesus.

Now, we listen to Brother Andrew, who points out the little boy and his meal. Verse 9 gives us his words and then his thinking: "But what is this little amount of food in the midst of so many?" Andrew's question is "Can we feed them all with this little bit?" Doubt sets in before the words are out of his mouth. Both of these disciples provide us with a startling view of us, the church, with the responsibility of stewardship of the poor. There is a challenge set before us with both of the disciples. Are we so overwhelmed by the needs around us and the tasks before us that we feel helpless, like Philip? Or do we sincerely recognize the gifts among us, like Andrew, and yet fail to see how God can use our meager offerings to make extraordinary blessings available for "all of these"? Can we feed them all?

The good news is found in the nameless little boy who shared his lunch. He knew it was only enough for him. He realized that his mom prepared it for him. He too could see the vast numbers of hungry people around him. Yet he offered up what he had. He shared what he had. He gave what he had. He did not put limits on what the Master Teacher could do with his offering. He did not speculate on what folks would say about what he offered. He did not hesitate, in the face of so many, to offer what little he had to share. And it was more than enough!

Children are willing to believe in miracles. Children have great imaginations. Children don't have adult realities and logical, scientific rationalizations that tell them certain things are impossible. If Jesus, the Teacher, the Healer, the Rabbi, whom they had walked miles to hear, wanted a lunch in the midst of all these folks, who was he to question? Jesus asked for help. The child offered Jesus his lunch. It was more than enough!

The crowd that was close enough to hear this encounter laughed at the foolishness of this little lad. Why, he had scarce resources. He was dealing with a microlunch for the multitudes. The people laughed at his audacity. They mocked his offering. They felt that the little boy was really naïve. Jesus did not laugh. He accepted the offering from the hands of this little boy.

Look at verses 11–12: "Jesus took the loaves, and when he had given thanks, he distributed them to those who were seated; so also the fish, as much as they wanted. When they were satisfied, he told his disciples, 'Gather up the fragments.'"

Doesn't it sound like communion? Isn't this the idea for community? In the breaking of the bread and the taking of the cup don't we participate in the body of Christ ministry that says, "Yes! We can feed them all"? Communion is the taking of what has been given unto us and offering a tad bit of it to others. This is why we tithe. God gives us all we receive.

God demands that we return 10 percent of our income as tithes. God multiplies the 10 percent we bring and there is enough to feed them all. The other day I was reading a magazine article about the way that Americans eat. It showed that if we only left a portion of our foods on our plates each time we sit to a meal, at the end of the month we would have lost weight without dieting. I'm a living witness that giving up a little drops a lot off the hips.

I'm a serious victim of conspicuous consumption. I didn't know how much "stuff" I had until we made our last move. From 9:30 in the morning until 2:30 in the afternoon, with only a lunch break in between, I stood at the top of the stairs directing the movers with boxes and things. Around 2:30 I couldn't take it anymore. I was overwhelmed. I asked the lead mover, as if he had sneaked "stuff" onto the van without my knowledge, "How much more do you have?" He replied, "about five more feet of boxes."

Did I need all of that stuff? Of course not. Could others make use of what I have bought, paid for, and would most likely never use again? Of course. Can we feed them all? Surely we can, if we simply offer a little of what we have unto God. Now, you know and I know that the real deal is that there were many other folks in that crowd who had food with them. Country folks don't go off without packing a lunch. I keep some peanut butter crackers in my attaché. For one never knows when or where you may get stuck.

One January day in Michigan, I left home to attend a T. D. Jakes evangelistic preaching festival, with the weather warning of a blizzard approaching. I stopped at one of the local supermarkets, with my tote bag on my arm. I bought fried chicken wings, potato salad, rolls, graham cracker cookies, a chicken salad sandwich, bottled water, and a jar of orange juice, just in case. I spent so much until I called Chuck, laughing, as I went on to church. For just in case, I wasn't going to be hungry and the people around me could have some too.

So I know that the people there had food. Yet nobody else said anything. They were all afraid they would lose what they had brought. But the little boy offered his whole meal and went down in the history book of the church.

Perhaps it was the generosity of this little boy that brought out into the open all of the hidden resources. Perhaps it was simply another miracle of love divine. Jesus cares about the full welfare of the people. And food is a basic necessity.

Can we feed them all? If we don't put limits on what God can do we can feed them all. Can we feed them all? If we don't hold back what it is God has given us to share we can feed them all. Can we feed them all? If we can envision offering our little unto Jesus Christ we can feed them all. For it is in love, compassion, forgiveness, and mercy that Jesus fed the multitude, including the women and the children. We have a hard time believing it, but God feeds us so miraculously, loves us so extravagantly, and forgives us so completely that we can willingly offer our best resources, knowing it will be enough.

Can we feed them all? If we come to Jesus Christ with childlike trust, wide-eyed expectations, and reckless faith, we will see the miracles of life. When we are willing to loosen our tight grip on what we think we possess, if we simply offer up our lunch, God yearns to do marvelous and wonderful things among us and with us. For Jesus is concerned about our welfare. And he died to feed us all!

This week, eat a little less. Offer something to the food bank in your community. Give a day's lunch money to a homeless person and fast until dinner. Take an extra sandwich to share with a bag lady or a homeless man. Collect all those personal items you have brought home from hotels and get them into the hands of community Christian service organizations or shelters.

As a matter of fact, let's start today! Take something out of your pocket or purse, something off of your person, and give it away the very next time you leave your house. Come on, if we honestly begin to share, like our little brother—YES! We can feed them all!

8

NEW LIFE DECISIONS

Responsible Discipleship

JOHN 20:1–18

It's the same old story! The women awoke to the start of another day filled with pain and with regrets. The women, charged with the responsibility of preparing dead bodies for the journey to "the other side," had work before them that had no pleasure in it at all. The women got up, despite the nasty business of working with another dead body, and, as a group, they prepared to move towards the tomb of Jesus, the son of their sister and their friend, Mary.

What if they had decided to stay put and to wallow in their common despair? It's the same old story! One woman in particular was searching for a "lost" man. She was doing what so many of us do, crying, looking, and grieving. The woman was out in a dead place, alone, searching for a dead man. The woman was not with her group of companions. The woman had left the place of safety with locked doors and bolted windows. The woman had stepped over the edge.

The woman had broken out of the box. The woman had moved past cultural expectations. What if she had decided to stay with the crowd and feel that the mission before her was impossible?

Depending upon what book of the gospel that you read during the season of Lent that prepares us for Easter, the women are always there. Easter is all about our precious times of resurrection, getting up and starting all over again! Easter is our time of new beginnings and our exchange of stagnant death for the opportunity of living the abundant life. What if we, like the collective of Easter women, decided to move past the "stone" that is in our life at this moment? What if we made the conscious decision to press past the conventional methods and strategies that are not working and take that leap of faith to follow our hearts?

Just imagine, with me, for a little while, what if, like these our sisters, we take these precious times together and make some new life decisions?

Both Matthew and Mark tell of a woman who dared to move past the "what ifs" of her culture. She knew that it was uncommon for a woman to be in a mixed crowd of dining men. She knew that her reputation had made her not the sort of woman that a rabbi would want in his company. Yet she had come to a discerning realization that even the male disciples did not have among themselves.

Our sister knew that Jesus had been born to die! She also discerned that his time was short. So she decided to offer him the very best that she had. She burst into a room of critical men to pour sweet anointing oil upon the head of Jesus. In the midst of the commotion, Jesus said: "Why are you giving this woman a hard time? She has just done something wonderfully significant for me . . . what she really did was anoint me for burial . . . wherever in the whole world the message is preached, what she has just done is going to be remembered and admired" (Matt. 26:10–13; Mark 14:6–9). What if she had listened to the critical voices in her head?

This is a woman who knelt down and dared to call the disciples, by her actions, to say, "Oh, come and let us adore him who is Jesus Christ, our Savior!" For her bravery, her discernment, and her willingness to risk public humiliation, Jesus gave her the highest accommodation in history. "She will be remembered and admired!" This is the sister who shows us the ministry of service to others that gets immediate results, so unexpected and so blessed beyond imagination.

Luke's account of the events following Jesus' death, in chapter 24, describes the bodaciousness of four women who discovered the very first Easter resurrection! They left the tomb and broke the news of all this to the eleven and the rest, but the apostles didn't believe a word of it, and thought they were making it all up (Luke 24:10–11). What if these women had done like we have been taught and had kept quiet, covenanted to hold their secret, and stayed in their "place" as those who were both oppressed and viewed as invisible?

These are the very women who got up and moved out into the cold dawn of a new morning, with the full reality that a massive stone was blocking their entrance to the body of Jesus. Yet they moved forth with determination toward their common goal. Stones are facts of life. Stones, blocking our way, are not new to us. Stones, obstacles that we press past and move around quickly, are in the history of our foremothers. For, in community, this group felt that they would simply trust God to handle what they could not achieve. And God surely did! For our God is an expert in removing stones!

Finally, in chapter 20 of John's Gospel, we have the portrait of a single woman, Mary Magdalene, coming to the tomb early in the morning while it was yet dark. Mary Magdalene, like many of us, is in the dark hunting for a man that she loved. She's in a graveyard, the place of the nonliving! She's searching for a body that cannot do anything for her. She's looking for a man who needs her ministry. There she runs into a male gardener. This places the sister in a garden spot! And here we need to pause for a minute.

In the very first garden the woman, Eve, was given a harsh penalty for neglecting to follow God's command to not "eat from the tree in the middle of the garden." Eve's name has been sullied, branded, and made mockery of ever since. What we often neglect is the fact that Adam, her tall, dark, and silent husband, was standing right with her (Gen. 3:6). For her deed of disobedience she received both a curse and a blessing. Eve was to be made subject to her husband and to bear her children in pain. The gift was that her seed would crush the head of the serpent. Her "seed" was Jesus, planted by the power of the Holy Spirit and not according to the "seed" of a man.

Jesus, known in Holy Scripture as the second Adam, discovers a little, weeping woman, Mary Magdalene, searching for a dead man in a garden. This makes a woman traditionally portrayed by the church as having a horrible reputation, a smeared name, and a broken spirit the "second" Eve! For a garden scene is being ready to be played out again. A garden curse is about to be reversed. A garden downfall is about to be lifted up for the whole world to see. This garden scene is the emancipation of all womanhood! What if the little woman had followed the dictates of her society? What if she had stayed home and never gone to the garden?

If the church tradition for identifying Mary Magdalene with the woman caught in adultery is true, then this single woman with a bad name was given the responsibility to go and to tell hidden brothers and sisters, yet locked in the upper room that Jesus Christ was up! This woman who had done the unimaginable was charged with going to spread the message of resurrection! She was told not to be weepy and clingy. She was told not to continue her role of being a touchy-feely woman. But she was challenged to go and to make a permanent, positive impact upon the world with her words, her insight, and her commission! And she did! Thanks be unto God!

She might well have said these words, which I share with you from the e-mail circuit:

This is the beginning of a new day. God has given me this day to use as I will. I can waste it or use it for good. What I do today is important, because I'm exchanging a day of my life for it. When tomorrow comes, this day will be gone forever, leaving in its place something that I have traded for it. I want it to be gain, not loss; good, not evil; success, not failure; in order that I shall not regret the price I paid for it. (Anonymous)

As we celebrate again this message of Easter and resurrection that prepares us for Mother's Day, when we make it our business to honor all of those various counsels of people who have been the nurturing mothers in our lives, we have serious decisions to make, dear sisters. We can allow these precious times to pass us by, doing the same old things, the same old ways. Or, we can dare to imitate the biblical role models set before us in scripture and chose new and abundant life.

We can gather as groups of sisters and decide to do something that is necessary for our communities. For there are many needy children, many hurting men and women, who have allowed the stones of life to keep them down, buried in despair. When a group of us get together, in the name of the Risen Christ, things have to change.

It has always been the women in our communities who began the first schools and colleges and the first penny saving banks. We are the ones who have taken in the homeless, mothered the aliens among us, and been forced to care for those who didn't look like us! However, it is always in our serving others that God rolls away stones, gives us the strength to climb over them, and, when necessary, makes walking paths out of them as we have chipped away at them with our bare hands! What if we dare gather again this season?

This is an excellent season to call together a group of women and begin a book club, a study group, or a prayer band. Have you ever heard of the power of the ancient prayer bands? Try prayer and discover what happens for you. Remember that praying involves more than words!

You might want to do scripture praying, where you select a passage, read it, and pause. Read it again, and then ask what words stand out for the group. Pause. Finally, read it the third time. Then ask again for the words that penetrate the spirit. Watch the discussion take on a life of its own.

A group of women meet with me on Mondays at WomanSpace for what we call Book and Bible. We choose a work of fiction and allow it to pull us into what God has to say about matters that arise. One of the books that lasted for almost three months was one of the shortest in number of pages. We selected *Showing Mary* by Renita Weems.[1] The discussion, the sister-to-sister care, and the prayers that arose from the book were overwhelming. Another awesome work is *When Twilight Comes* by Gwynne Forster.[2]

Or we can chose to follow the leading of the Holy Spirit and do like Mary Magdalene—go off, individually, seeking what we can discover, while walking through the darkness of not knowing with certainty where we will end. Mary Magdalene told the "gardener" to just tell her where they had laid him and that she would go and get the body, which would have been very heavy, being dead weight.

Can you hear her self-confidence? Can you feel the love that overwhelmed her, causing her to know with assurance that she could do what she had committed to doing? She realized that this was a "new day." She understood that the pain of yesterday was over. And she made a conscious decision that she was not going to waste the new day before her.

The issue for you and for me is one of growing on and not simply going on! Spiritual growth and development is our only goal here. We celebrate that God allowed these women to be chosen to minister in this season of resurrection. We have joined them, in a community of sistership that is destined to continue our forward movement. For even as we write, read, and pray together, the Spirit of resurrection is calling each of us again. Last year is dead and gone.

Yesterday has passed. This, a new day, lies before us in all sort of pregnant possibilities. What will we do with this present?

What if we dared to journey past our stones? What if we dared to move through the dark nights of our souls, into the bright "Son" of a new dawn? What if our divine destiny awaited us as we rose to seek new places in God? The choice before us is to take a leap of faith, to risk what seems certain in order to achieve what feels impossible.

The God of all times awaits our decision to get up and to move out into a waiting world that continues to need our message that Jesus lives! As the hymnist Alfred Ackley voiced, "You ask me how I know he lives. He lives within my heart!"[3]

9

A WOMAN GOD CAN USE

Responsible Forward Movement

1 SAMUEL 1:4–20

I f you give the best of your service; telling the world that the Savior has come, and then another sister gets on your last nerve, can God yet read your mind and say, "Girlfriend, well done?" If you have tried, and failed in your trying, and your heart is so scarred from the work that you have done, and another sister steals your ideas and leaves you off her program, can God yet read your mind and say, "Girlfriend, well done?"

We are just the women that God can use. We are just the sisters that are needed. We are ready, willing, and able to help make the program a success, but what do we do when our enemy is another sister? The issue of women not supporting each other is something that we only want to talk about in a closed group meeting, on the telephone, or in the parking lot. The sister who is envious, jealous, and a back-stabber is not one whose name we want to call aloud among the sisterhood. But the real truth is that we all have a sister who we know will steal our stuff, sabotage our plans, and wreck our reserved nerves.

My wreck began in March of one year. I had planned, orchestrated, and chaired a Citywide Women's History Month Revival. Nothing like this had ever been held in my community. I wanted only the very best clergywoman to represent the ministry. I wanted my city to see beauty. I wanted my city to experience beauty. I wanted my city to know that for years, there had been women pastors in the Baptist denomination. I wanted them to experience educational excellence, mixed with the Holy Spirit's anointing. This was a first-time event. It had to be outstanding. Therefore, I invited The Very Rev. Brenda J. Little to come to Grand Rapids, Michigan. I picked her up and made sure that she was well taken care of—she stayed at the airport Hilton Hotel—and well paid. She came to the pulpit each night wearing a designer robe and walking on five-inch designer heels. Brenda put women in ministry on the map in a very conservative town. Brenda preached so powerfully that one of the male clergy asked me if I would bring her back to Michigan the next year.

He wanted to host the next year's Citywide Women's History Month Revival. As the time approached for me to contact Brenda concerning her availability, I called the pastor to insure what it was that he wanted. We discussed the program and we agreed that I would teach nightly at 7:00–8:00 P.M. My teaching would be followed by Rev. Little's preaching. I was sure that she would "slay the house," "wreck the city," and declare the Word of God with beauty, power, and anointing each night. Are you with me?

There was only one little stipulation as we moved towards the Citywide Women's History Month Revival. I had to work with a woman who was the chairperson of the women's ministry at his church. I didn't think that it would be a problem because I knew the sister. At one time, she had complained of her financial dilemma and I, being financially able, sent her an unsolicited monetary love offering. I really felt that she and I had a good understanding between us. Lord, was I ever surprised!

I called the sister and told her that her pastor had given me permission to come and be a blessing to the women. I shared that her church would host the second annual Citywide Women's History Month Revival and that she and I needed to work together to make this happen. She listened. When I gave her the dates, she hesitated. She said that she had considered inviting her niece to preach at her church during the same time. I therefore asked if we might perhaps organize a Saturday prayer breakfast or luncheon and have her niece be the keynote preacher. She told me that her niece was not "that type of speaker." She said that her niece "went forth" and could not be confined to time constraints. I asked her to give me some clarification on what "went forth" meant.

My clergy sister said to me, "Doc, I'm glad that you have gotten an education. But we need something more." I could tell right then that she was not happy with me. Yet, I pressed on for resolution in an effort to move forward together. I gave her the plan that her pastor and I had developed. And I said that I'd agreed to teach each night. She listened until I got through, and, of course, she told me that she would have to pray about the matter and call me back the next day.

True to her word, she called the next day and left a message on my voice mail. "Dr. Hollies, we have met and prayed. We have decided to not go along with your format. God bless you." I called her pastor, who supported her decision. I left the idea alone. But (and it's a very big but!) the very next week, there were flyers and announcements being made all over the city of Grand Rapids about the Citywide Women's History Month Revival. God knows, I was shocked and surprised. This sister kept my same theme and title. She only changed the format to feature her niece, who "went forth." And did she ever network!

She got the praying women to gather. They had a huge luncheon with all the "first ladies" in the city, who brought women from their churches to plan the event. They included suburban congregations and those of other cultures. The men of their church handled valet parking. They had various congregations assigned to bring meals for receptions after the evening worships. They advertised for vendors. It was a big event in the town. There, however, was one problem. I was never invited to any event. The pastor saw me at the Dr. Martin Luther King Jr. Day celebration and asked if I had received any information from my sister clergy. Then he said, "I wonder why she didn't send you an invitation?"

Sisters, I was pushed completely out of the way. I was rubbed from the picture. I was eliminated like garbage. I was told that there was standing room only during the first night of the event. I was told that during the first night, the men had to give up their seats and encircle the walls. I was told that the praise and worship service during the first night was awesome. I was also told that when the woman's niece began to "go forth," the people got up and left the sanctuary. I got a call about 10:00 that night from a friend who said, "Doc, it's a good thing that your name was not associated with this mess." I got another call that said, "Sis, the ministry of women has been set back at least fifteen years."

Yes, I showed up the second night to experience our sister "going forth." She was hurt that the people had walked out the night before. She was angry that folks had called the pastor and complained that she never opened the Bible and gave them a scripture. She said that when we left, if we couldn't say something good, to not say anything. So there is no further report about her and her "going forth." If when you give the best of your service, telling the world that the Savior has come, and then another sister gets on your last nerve, can God yet read your mind and say, "Girlfriend, well done?"

If you have tried, and failed in your trying, and your heart is so scarred from the work that you have done, and then another sister steals your ideas and leaves you off her program, can God yet read your mind and say, "Girlfriend, well done?" We are just the women that God can use. We are the sisters who are needed. We are ready, willing, and able to help make the program a success, but what do we do when our enemy is another sister? The Word of God has something for us to reflect upon. The Word of God has a record of this scene being played out, over and over. The Word of God has some wisdom that we need to chew on and to remember in 1 Samuel 1:4–20.

This is the very familiar story of Hannah, a woman called and chosen by God to bring forth Samuel, who would become the very first priest and prophet in Israel. She was a woman, a daughter, and a wife. But she was unhappy. As a matter of fact, Hannah was miserable. If you want to be honest, the sister was wrestling with big time depression. She did not feel like she'd been called by God. She didn't feel like she'd been chosen by God. She didn't feel like she was being loved by God. As we enter into her life's story, we find a woman who felt "dissed"—dismissed and desolate. She was a dearly beloved woman. She'd been given a double portion of her husband's priestly sacrifice. She was the first wife.

She was in charge of the house. Her husband treated her like a queen. He asked her, "Am I not more to you than ten sons?" Still we find Sista Hannah weeping, not eating, and sitting deep down in a pity-pot with a broken heart. For Hannah had not been able to have a child. So her husband had married a second wife, Peninnah, who bore sons.

It seemed that Peninnah's mission in life was to mock, make fun of, and to add misery to Hannah's life. This seemed to be a repeated scene, year after year. For verse 6 says, "Her rival used to provoke her severely, to irritate her, because the Lord had closed her womb." Who was responsible for Hannah's misery? It was the decision of God! In our pain, God has both a reason and a promise. In our pain, God has planted the seed to our tomorrow's praise. In our pain, God is preparing us for the destiny that is ours. We can't get to tomorrow's assignment without first stopping to acknowledge, to learn from, to grow and further develop as we are taught by the very painful place where we are located today. "The Lord had closed Hannah's womb."

We find it difficult to believe that God places us in tough spots. We can't get our heads around the fact that a loving Creator would permit and allow something harsh or something horrible to happen to us. We want to bind Satan. We want to touch and agree with others for our deliverance. We want to fast and pray and have our painful situations go away as fast as possible. But verse 7 of the text says, "So, it went on year by year; as often as she went up to the house of the Lord, she used to provoke her." This was not a fast, easy microwave test. This was not a "speak-to-the-mountain-and-watch-it-move" situation. This was not an instant deliverance test of faith. But because Hannah had a unique, particular, and special role in the overall plan of God, she had to endure. Hannah had to learn how to serve God under pressure. Hannah had to learn how to serve God with perseverance. Hannah had to learn all of the lessons; she had to pass all of the tests. And she had to do it in such a way that God could be pleased with her responses to a messy life.

Hannah was the woman for this hour. Hannah was a lesson in waiting. Hannah was a woman who had great anxiety, vexation, depression, and distress, yet she passed God's test of time. Hannah teaches women who are called and chosen by God that we must learn, in every situation, how to keep right on getting up, wiping our weeping eyes, and stepping, by faith, to "next."

Verse 9 declares that Hannah rose. Hannah got up. Hannah decided that life was tough, but she was tougher. Hannah decided that there was something else that she could do. Hannah went to the Temple and began to pray. Her prayer is the first recorded text of a woman speaking to the Almighty in the canon of Scriptures. Hannah's prayer has an element that we hear again in Mary's Magnificat. Hannah's faith was anchored in the God who comes in due season—for God does not come until we have mastered all the lessons. Hannah had to learn that all that was shiny was not gold. It looked like Peninnah was having the last laugh. It seemed like the strong male offspring that Peninnah had borne Elkanah were destined to be his only heirs. It seemed as if time had passed Hannah by and now she was down for the count. It seemed as if God had forsaken her, forgotten about her, and just left. But Hannah continued to trust God and she continued to pray.

To pray is to pour out one's soul before the throne. To pray is to tell God all about the innermost feelings of our soul. To pray is to ask God to "remember me." To pray is to ask God for favor. Deeply distressed, weeping bitter tears that spoke volumes to God, Hannah, the Bible says, presented herself before God (verse 9a). When we pray, we need only use minimal words.

God read Hannah's countenance. God read Hannah's spirit. God read Hannah's tears. God reads the wave of our hand. God reads our moans and groans. God reads the candles that we light. God reads the footsteps that we take as we walk the floor, wordless and bereft. All that we have to do is become "the present," holy and acceptable unto God. God met Hannah when she presented herself at the temple. For God was there, all the time, waiting for Hannah to learn all of the lessons and to dare to pray.

To pray is to ask God, as David did, in Psalms 119:32–48 to "'Teach me, O Lord, the way of your statures, and I will observe it to the end. Give me understanding, that I may keep your law and observe it with my whole heart. Lead me in the path of your commandments, for I delight in it. Turn my heart to your decrees, and not to selfish gain. Turn my eyes from looking at vanities; give me life in your ways. Confirm to your servant your promise, which is for those who fear you. Turn away the disgrace that I dread, for your ordinances are good. See, I have longed for your precepts; in your righteousness give me life."

Hannah learned that her difficulties prepared her for a greater victory. Hannah learned that her confusion prepared her for greater clarity of God's vision for her life and that of her son. Hannah learned that what she perceived as failure was only a lesson on her way to good success. Hannah learned that her poverty of spirit prepared her for prosperity. Hannah learned that Peninnah's criticism prepared her for the acceptance of Eli, the high priest, as the voice of God. Hannah learned that her heavy pain had prepared her for the greatest of joy. Hannah's anger at both God and Peninnah prepared her for the ability to forgive others. Hannah's ignorance about how God is directing each and every one of our steps prepared her to receive a far greater truth than she had ever imagined. Hannah had to learn that being lonely prepared her with the capacity to receive God's amazing love. Hannah loved God so much that she offered back her son, the very thing that she had longed for the most. Hannah did what the average Christian woman will not do. She was willing to get up and "bust a move!" Twice the scripture declares that "Hannah rose." In verse 9, while in her depressed state, she got up. Then, after her confrontation with Eli, and receiving the assurance that her prayers had been heard, she rose early in the morning, says verse 19. The word "rose," indicates a new intention to work despite the obstacles.

The word "rose" means that she was going to keep on pushing past the limits that she felt. The word "rose" means that she was willing to risk being vulnerable again. She was willing to try something new, something different, something unusual—being a woman who dared to worship near a priest. Most of us are habitual conference, workshop, and seminar attendees. We attend willingly to get new knowledge, information, and techniques. We pay for the opportunity to get new notebooks, new ad books, and new program souvenir books. Then we take all these things home and stack them on the shelf. There is no change in our lives. There is no transformation.

There is no more forward movement from where we were before we registered for the workshop! But Hannah says to each of us, called and chosen by God, we have to be about getting up, moving on, and daring to name a new ministry focus.

We will all discover that Peninnah will not change. We are the ones who must change! We cannot remain in the same state as we were before. It's time to wipe our weeping eyes, to put our hands on our hips, and to allow our backbones to move us on toward our destiny. When Sista Hannah got home, different, transformed, and assured that a hearing and answering God was on her side, things changed. God remembered her in due time. I have come to announce to you, my beloved sistas, that this is due time.

Hannah had a mission. Her mission was to make a baby that would bless the realm of God. This is your mission and it's mine. Our mission is to give birth to something spiritual that will spread the ministry of Christ. So we have to know our purpose. We have to have a mission statement to help us stay focused and in our field of expertise. Some businesses fail because they try to do too many things. Often we fail, when we don't know where God has called us to be most effective in ministry. None of us can do everything! Yet each of us has been called and chosen to do something specific in ministry. Our pain points the way to our ministry. For the same God who called us has now prepared us to share the very lessons that we have learned with others.

We must get this last lesson from Sista Hannah. Before her situation changed, Hannah changed. Look at verse 18b. "Then the woman went to her quarters, ate and drank with her husband, and her countenance was sad no longer." Before her situation changed, Hannah's attitude changed. Before her situation changed, Hannah's emotional state changed. Before her situation changed, her spiritual attitude changed. Verse 19 says that Sista got up the next morning and worshiped before the Lord.

We each need a personal mission statement that will guide us. We need to acknowledge our greatest, most longstanding pain that holds for us the seed to our destiny. We have to be willing to pour out our hearts before God and before each other. We have to get clarity about how we can move in a new direction. Then we will become a witness to each other, like Eli, reminding one another that we can go forward with God's shalom.

Finally, we must ask God both to remember us and to have favor upon us. Everywhere there are women whom God longs to use. In every area of our life there are women who can help others to heal, to grow, to develop and to stretch towards their divine destiny. In every situation where we find ourselves, there are women who have learned their lessons, passed their tests, and now can assist others of us on the journey. God longs for us to use each other as resources.

First, I'm going to ask that you assume now a posture of prayer. I want you to sit quietly and remember your greatest pain. What has caused a hole in your spirit? What keeps you from moving ahead? Hannah wanted a son. What has God denied you over the years? I just want you to remember it. I want you to reflect upon it. Then I want you to silently present it to God. At the end of your prayer time, beseech God to "remember me and grant me favor."

Now, in a journal, write down one word that describes your greatest pain(s). You are not going to give details. Just write down your chronicle of pain. After this process, answer this question: What has been most helpful and most healing for you on the journey? In as few words as possible, write how God has reached out to you in the midst of your pain. Eli spoke to Hannah. Who has reached you? Write this down in your chronicle of pain. The last question will be: What will I do to help other sisters discover healing from my type of pain? At this point you are describing different types of personal ministry opportunities that you know are needed across the world.

Hannah named her son Samuel, "for she said, I have asked him of the Lord." What name will you give to the ministry that your pain has led you to construct? My mission in life is to teach the people of God. Like Hannah I have had to undergo a change and grow through some hard lessons in order to teach others. Life for me "ain't been no crystal stair!"

I am clear that my ministry is devoted to the ninety-nine who have already committed to Jesus Christ. I'm also clear that my ministry is primarily aimed at the women in this population. This allows me to stay focused. I don't evangelize. I'm on the side of God that encourages those who are hanging on by a thread to hang on. You have to know your audience. What side are you on? Do you enjoy soul winning? Do you enjoy training others in the way that they should go? If yes, then, that's an entirely different audience from mine.

I am persuaded that my purpose from God and my mission on earth is to teach the people of God by writing, preaching, and teaching the life lessons that God insists that I learn! If you are on a mission, you will need a mission statement. Why? Because a mission statement has movement. A mission statement has to focus on how the mission will be directed. A verb, an action word, is required in a mission statement. Take the time now to write your personal mission statement. Now move forward, Sista Hannah, and allow the world to watch you strut your stuff!

LOOKING OUT FOR YOUR OWN BEST WELFARE

Thrift is about critical decision making and pacing. Old-style thriftiness is about moderation, prioritizing needs, cultivating patience, and learning about delayed gratification. As Terrie Williams says in *A Plentiful Harvest*:

> Debt is slavery, and there are too many of us who are slaves, living on the credit-card plantation. In order to move forward we have to break the cycle with these four steps:

1. Communicate: Talk to someone who can help you to free yourself from the cycle of debt. Financial counselors are a great resource. They can assist in developing a plan to renegotiate interest rates and terms of your debt. Work with a counselor to develop a budget that you can live with, and then stick to it.

2. Get used to spending cash: Put the credit cards away! Give them to a friend you trust and don't take them back until they are all paid off. Better yet, cut them up. Keep one if you must, but always pay it off at the end of the month.

3. Remember your income: Whenever you consider making a purchase, think about your income first. What is your net income (after taxes) per month? If you buy this thing, in cash, will you be able to pay the rent and utilities, buy groceries, and so on? Your income is your reality. You haven't won the lottery, so you must discipline yourself to spend within your means. "Your means" is no fantasy number—it is your net income, plain and simple. Keep a running tab of every purchase you make for the next month. Try to monitor your spending so you still have at least a small portion of your monthly income at the end of the month.

4. Look for ways to save money: Avoid calling directory assistance. Make long distance calls during off-peak hours. Don't let your checking or savings account dip below the amount designated by your bank. Avoid late penalties by paying your credit cards on time. Use coupons when grocery shopping. Do you really need cable television? If not, cut it off. Turn off lights and water when not using them. Call around and see if you can get a better rate on your automobile insurance. Try to lower your credit-card interest rate by moving your business to another card. They'll often lower rates to get your business.[1]

Sista Hannah, if you want to have a healthy, happy, and productive life, you must get out of debt. If you're sick and tired of being a slave on the credit-card plantation, cut up your cards and pay down those balances. If you want a financial legacy to pass on to your children, protect their investment by working toward debt freedom today!

10

YOUR ANSWER, PLEASE?

Responsible Harvest

JOHN 1:1–5, 14

The children of a great couple decided to send them on a cruise for their fiftieth anniversary celebration. This couple had spent many years of being good stewards of their resources. You could even call them tight. But they went on the cruise and came back refreshed.

The children gathered to take them home and to see the many pictures they had shot while away. As they looked and listened to their parents, one said, "I don't see any photograph of you with the captain." "We never saw the captain," they replied. "Well, on every cruise there is a captain's dinner. Where are those pictures?" There was a space of silence. Finally, one of the children said, "Mom, Dad, your answer, please?" To which the dad replied, "We packed snacks in our luggage and didn't want you kids to have to pay for our food too. We never ate outside of our stateroom."

These nice people went on a cruise and missed half of the fun of eating in the fabulous dining room. They missed calling for room service and the midnight buffets—they never experienced any of it. They were trying to save what had already been paid for. These were nice folks. These were economical folks. But these were some ignorant folks! Had they dared to read the cruise brochure, they would have learned that the meals were included in the cost of the cruise. Had they dared to read the cruise brochure, they would have seen that they never had to leave their room if that was their choice. Room service is provided and gladly delivered. Because they had not read the cruise brochure, they lived beneath their privilege as paid guests of the cruise ship.

These nice people are so like too many of us. Too many of us in the church live beneath our privilege as people of the Ruler of Rulers. Jesus Christ is the Ruler to the glory of God. And you and I are heirs and joint heirs of an everlasting realm. We have the Omnipotent, Omnipresent, and Omniscient Sovereign on our side. We serve Jesus Christ, who was sacrificed for our sin. He was betrayed by one of his own. He was hung on a cross, pierced in his side, suffered, bled, and died to justify us and to set us free from the dominion of sin. Then Jesus Christ rose again! He got up as the victor over sin, death, and hell to win the privilege for us to have a personal and intimate relationship with the Almighty. When Jesus Christ ascended into heaven, where he now sits on God's right hand, he became dedicated to interceding, cheerleading, and rooting for us to win, to rule, and to be victorious in our daily lives.

Jesus Christ didn't stop there, but waited fifty days and sent back the Holy Spirit, who dares to live in us, to pray for us, to interpret our groans, to read our tears, to lead us, to guide us, and to direct us into all truth, and then to remind us of the Jesus way. People of God, we have it going on! God is for us. We have Jesus who freed us. We have the Holy Spirit in us and all of heaven's angels on our side. We have the promises that we are always above and never beneath. We are the head and never the tail. We can walk through water and not drown. We can be placed in fiery furnaces and come out without the smell of smoke. When we wait on God, our strength is renewed as eagles; we can run and not be weary; we can walk and not faint. No weapon formed against us can prosper. No foe can defeat us. No storm can sweep us away. For our souls are anchored in God! It's all good. It's all great. It's all guaranteed. So the question is, what have we done with all of this sanctified power?

The question is, how much difference have we made in the world that we touch? The question is, why are our world, our community, and our homes so filled with chaos, turmoil, and drama? Your answer, please? Daughter of God, every fall we celebrate the ingathering season in America. The farmer gathers in the crop. The earth has done its job for another year. The spring rains watered the ground, the summer sun caused growth, and now the fall will reap a harvest. Even dope dealers, as evil and satanic as they are, expect a yield of the poppy fields during the fall ingathering. And they will produce. So surely Christ the King is waiting to see the crop that we will bring. What have we done this past week with all that we have been provided? Your answer, please? The gospel of John seems to pivot on the question, who is this Jesus whom we serve?

The good news of Jesus begins in John's record with a song. It's a hymn to the Living Word of God. For, "In the beginning was the Word, and the Word was with God, and the Word was God. He was in the beginning with God. All things came into being through him, and without him not one thing came into being. What has come into being in him was life, and the life was the light of all people. The light shines in the darkness, and the darkness did not overcome it. . . . And the Word became flesh and lived among us, and we have seen his glory, the glory as of God's only son, full of grace and of truth" (John 1:1–5, 14).

John gives us a narration of a three-year ministry of signs and wonders. He tells us that Jesus is the great "I Am." He is the Door. He is the Gate. He is the Bread. He is the Living Water. And he is the Good Shepherd who laid down his life for the sheep. John gives us many views of different women, and how important they are to Jesus. John provides us with portraits of a praying Jesus who walks into a graveyard and declares: "God, I thank you that you have heard me pray. I knew that you always heard me, but I said this for the benefit of the people standing here, that they may believe that you sent me." Then, this praying Jesus calls a dead man to come forth and to be released.

John shows us a calling Jesus. This is a relationship-building Jesus, who makes water into wine at a wedding—where both the bride and the groom are about to be embarrassed. This is a healing Jesus, who has to go and see about a woman with an achy-breaky heart and a bad reputation. After a lengthy dialogue with Jesus, she leaves rejoicing. Her rejoicing woos the town to come and see a man who told her every thing that she had done. And never once did he condemn her.

This is a radical and an angry Jesus, who clears folks out of the Temple for taking advantage of the poor and making God's house into a den of thieves. This is a feeding Jesus, who takes a meal of crackers and sardines and opens an outdoor food pantry with the leftovers. This is a hurting Jesus. Many of his followers deserted him. They turned and walked away because they only wanted the fish and the loaves, and not the spiritual food that Jesus offered. We have a teaching Jesus in John. In the evening, the Jewish leaders also sneaked in to get a Word. This is a heart fixing, mind regulating, spirit soothing, and death defying Jesus. It is the Jesus who stooped down to write in the sand as he released the woman caught in adultery when no one could cast the first stone. This is an eye-opening Jesus who delivered a blind man from sightlessness, then told the church leaders, "If you were blind, you would not have sin. But now that you say, 'We see,' your sin remains" (John 9:41).

This is an anointed Jesus. This is the Jesus who was wept over and adored by a sinful woman whom the world despised, a woman who anointed his feet with costly oil and then wiped them with her hair. And Jesus told the angry disciples, "Leave her alone. She bought it so that she might keep it for the day of my burial" (John 12:7). When the boys could not see that the earthly days of Jesus were drawing to a close, there was a woman, an outsider. She was a disciple who saw Jesus' need and met it with her personal belongings. In John, we have an appreciative Jesus. In John, we have a Jesus who washes feet like a mother, and hosts a meal like a father. In John, we find a Jesus who promises the Holy Spirit as a comforter to be with us forever. In John, Jesus prays for himself. But more importantly, Jesus prays for us. "And now, I am no longer in the world, but they are in the world, and I am coming to you. Holy God, protect them in your name that you have given me, so that they may be one, as we are one" (John 17:11).

We also have in John a Jesus who is betrayed, arrested, and put on trial. As they try to trump up treason charges against him, he is dragged from Jewish judgment hall to judgment hall. Finally, they have to deliver Jesus to Pilate, the leader of the Roman government and the only one able to condemn him to death. Since Pilate knows full well that there is no legal, lawful, or binding reason for a sentence of death, he struggles, wrestles, and tries to find some way to fix the mess. Finally Pilate asks Jesus, "What have you done?" (John 18:35).

We all know and can witness to what Jesus has done for us! The question is what have we done for Jesus? Jesus was found guilty of doing good! That was the only charge that they had against him. "They" said that Jesus claimed to be "the son of God." Isn't that what we claim as Christian believers? So, as imitators, reflectors, and role models of a mighty God, what have we accomplished in the past week? Jesus Christ is the King of the world to come. Jesus Christ will judge the whole world. Jesus Christ will reign throughout eternity. Court is in session for each one of us called by his name. What have we done? Your answer, please? We are people of a covenant promise. By our new birth, we now belong to the realm of God. By the mandate of the great commission, we are to embody, enfold, and enflesh God in this present world. By the power of the Holy Spirit, we are the channels of healing. We are the instruments of hope. We are the vessels of justice. We are the ministers of reconciliation. All of this is part of our covenant relationship.

Honestly, it's all in the book that we call the Bible! When there are needs around us, we are to fill the needs. When there is turmoil, we are called to be the makers of peace. Where there is conflict, we are the ones to offer resolution. Where there is despair, we are the light. Where there is pain, we are the healing balm—for the realm of God is not something that is coming after awhile, bye and bye. No, the realm of God is you and me! So what have we done recently? Your answer, please? What activity did you engage in last week that brought light to a dismal situation? What community matter was your prayer concern last week? What child, besides your own family members, experienced your care, your outreach, or your advocacy? What did you do for a homeless person? Who was sick and you went to visit, call, or send a card or note? What national issue or international concern did you take before God's throne in prayer? Your answer, please?

We have all the tools to do all of the above! We have every resource to be effective ministers in the world! We've been saved from sin. We've been justified by faith. We've been washed in the blood. We've been liberated by the new covenant. We've been filled with the Holy Spirit. Each of us is a bona fide member of the church of Jesus Christ. So, what have we done to be the evidence? Your answer, please? Whenever we dare to pray the Lord's Prayer, we do petition God, "May your realm come on earth as it is in heaven." Well, the realm of God arrived with the death, burial, and resurrection of Jesus Christ.

The realm of God is now living within you and me. It's a realm of love, justice, generosity, and joy. It's a realm where chains are broken, prison doors are opened, and justice rolls down like a mighty river, through our combined ministries of service to the world. The realm of God is where our tears are welcomed and our laughter is a medicine. It's a realm where no one has to beg for crumbs, but, at the banquet table, we are all invited to feast from the Bread of Life until we want no more. It's a realm where love triumphs over division and where drugs, alcohol, and sexual promiscuity are arrested by God's amazing grace. It's a realm when our confusion is understood; where my gifts are put to use; where my questions are answered and what I need is supplied by people who can discern by spirit.

God's realm is where my grief is comforted and my pain is shared. It's a realm where there is no lack, for out of our tithing stewardship, there is always abundance in our storehouses. All people have to do is to ask. God's realm is where released prisoners, drug addicts, and reformed prostitutes can find welcome among the people of God. It's a place where the infant, the youngster, the teen, and the young adult can mix, mingle, and be accepted by those who have been around for as long as the building's dirt! For in God's realm, we are family!

In the realm of God there is room at the cross for all! It's a place where those who have been labeled nobodies become somebodies, precious, awesome, wondrously made, and dearly beloved. Thank God that this is an inclusive realm and there is a place for everybody to fit securely.

The realm of God is where the knee bent and the body bowed can stand up and be counted. It's a place where prayer is continually going up and blessings are continually being poured down. It's a realm whose maker and founder is Jehovah-Jirah, the Almighty Provider. It's a realm where love rules, so that there is affordable housing, effective recovery treatment, quality public education, and access to quality health care, done through the means of local church ministries. The realm of God has already come. It came one night, long ago when a baby was born in Bethlehem. It came with angels singing, stars twinkling, and witnesses galore. It's a realm that is continually breaking in more and more as you and I reach out to touch a dying world with our loving care.

It's a realm that walks the pavement of our city streets and the dusty rural roads. It's a realm that goes to marketplaces, shows up on our jobs, teaches and attends schools. It's a realm that dismantles abusive systems as it builds up strong Christians, week by week. These strong Christians return to the world, making permanent, positive impact upon their world. They make a lasting difference. The realm of God is coming again soon. Jesus Christ will break through the clouds and the dead in Christ will arise. As Gabriel blows the horn and the church is raptured into eternity, the realm of God will begin it's "forever" reign! And, just like Jesus had to stand before Pilate, one day we too will stand before the Potentate of Power. The records of our lives' work will be there, on pages bright and fair. There will be no typos, white-outs, erasures, or strikeovers to distract. Every deed done in our body will be evident and all of them will be examined!

We have been given all that we need to prepare for that day. The question on that day will be asked, "Beloved, what did you do to ensure that my realm was obvious, present, and visible in the world? What is it that you have accomplished for me? And the Mighty Ruler will ask, "Your answer, please?"

LOOKING OUT FOR YOUR OWN BEST WELFARE

The late, wonderful, and inspiring Ms. Oseola McCarty was the epitome of thrift and generosity. Miss McCarty had two skills; washing clothes and ironing clothes. After diligently saving her money over the many decades of her life, Miss McCarty donated a hundred fifty thousand dollars to the University of Southern Mississippi. Her generous gift stunned the nation. She didn't earn a lot, but through the disciplines of saving and thrift, she was able to amass quite a bit of money. She taught us that everyone can make a contribution, no matter how little or how much they have. Thanks to her life-long frugality, she made a difference in the lives of young students. Her legacy inspired a nation and it lives on. . . .

When you're suffering financially, it may feel like a hardship to give, but that's the time when you should really dig deep. The most powerful giving we'll ever do is when money is scarce. Ironically, that's when the blessings begin to flow. It's a faith thing. When you take a leap of faith and believe that all your needs will be met, no matter how empty your bank account may be, somehow the bills get paid. Giving money is an excellent spiritual discipline that develops faith. Selfishness is a real problem in our society, and giving is the cure. Selflessness is unpopular today; everywhere we're told to "get what's ours." But it's this very self-indulgence that is at the root of so much of the imbalance and stress that we suffer. A couple of hours of volunteering to a worthy cause could be just the thing to make your life more meaningful, which is so important to emotional health.

Giving reinforces your sense that you have enough. When you give, even a small amount, you'll find that you're still able to buy the things that you want, need, and desire. When you give, you feel like you have more than you had to begin with.[1]

11

SHE SHALL BE CALLED WOMAN!

God's Responsible Servant

GENESIS 1–2

She was nobly fashioned by the Divine Designer. She was created, not born. She sprang from the soil, but she had originated from above. She was fashioned out of dust, but she was inspired by the Triune's celestial breath. She was a friend to creatures, but she was the offspring of the Sovereign God. This beautiful new creature was placed in the delights of Eden. It was a beautiful and fertile garden, with light and pleasant occupation but responsible duties. She was gifted with immortality, intelligence, instincts, and speech.

She was God's crowning creation, who was invested with world dominion and trivial restrictions. She was not Jehovah-Elohim, who is supreme and ultimate. Nor was she simply an animal, created too low, without the power to think or to choose. According to the story in Genesis 2, she was the last of God's handiwork. Presumably, therefore, she is the best thing that God ever created! She is the crown of all visible creation. And woman is her name! She is God's most responsible servant!

God had created the very best home for her reception. God had made provision for her total maintenance. God gave her beauty to be appreciated, a build to be admired, and intellect to be respected. She was a gift and a present to the world. She was the added attraction. She was the cream of the crop. She was given claim to the full allegiance of her man. She was promised love, affection, wholesome sex, and protection from the beginning. Time, leisure, and approval were to be her allotted pleasures in life. She was to be held dear to the heart of her husband, for woman was her name!

Woman. The *isha* of Hebrew, taken from the word, *ish*, for man. Woman. The real glory of Adam, the man. Woman. The delight of heaven. For it is after her that the church of the Living God is named. Woman, the virginal and the pure, was made for clinging to and mating with one man. Adam was to fulfill her every sexual, emotional, and physical need. Woman. The mystery that gives blood like Jesus Christ. For without the shedding of innocent blood, there is no remission of sin. Yet, during her fertile days, when a woman stops her monthly bleeding, it's to create a new life. And when she has lived long enough to cease the monthly flow, that blood is stored within herself to be used as energy for re-inventing and re-creating herself!

Woman. The full wisdom of God. Woman. The fatal folly of fools. Woman. The joyful and the joyless astonishment of the human male world. For all across the world, woman is continually restrained, oppressed, and not understood. Woman. The indissoluble character in a marriage whose very image alone condemns the practice of polygamy and adultery. Woman. The softer and gentler character of nature. Woman. She will cry in both joy and pain. Woman. She will give and dares to take back. Woman. She is wife, mother, sister, friend, confidant, and foe, all wrapped into one flesh. Woman. She is bone, flesh, and intellect combined. Created last, so that she might be put first, and be called woman! An e-mail sent to me says it this way:

> She is a woman and at age three, she looks at herself and sees a queen. At age eight, she looks at herself and sees Cinderella. At age fifteen, she looks at herself and sees an ugly sister ("Mom I can't go to school looking like this!"). At age twenty, she looks at herself and sees "too fat/too thin, too short/too tall, too straight/too curly"—but decides she's going out anyway. At age thirty, she looks at herself and sees "too fat/too thin, too short/too tall, too straight/too curly"—but decides she doesn't have time to fix it, so she's going out anyway. At age forty, she looks at herself and sees "clean" and goes out anyway. At age fifty, she looks at herself and sees "I am woman" and goes wherever she wants to go. At age sixty, she looks at herself and reminds herself of all the people who can't even see themselves in the mirror anymore. Now, she goes out, set to conquer the world. At age seventy, she looks at herself and sees wisdom, laughter, and ability, and goes out and enjoys life. At age eighty, she doesn't even bother to look. She just puts on what suits her fancy and goes out to help season the rest of the world!

For ages the world has been asking the question found in Proverbs 31:10, "A capable wife who can find?" For ages men have been overlooking what's been right under their noses. For ages, our men of color have taken us for granted. We have been overlooked at home while they have taken their goods down the street or sought to find white, thin, and flat. We have taken care of them and put up with their mess along with their little, "look just like them" babies! Women of virtue have been among us all the time, responsible to the God of the Ages.

If not for women, there would be no Historic Black Colleges. If not for women, there would be no growing, thriving black churches. If not for women, there would never have been a savings and loan institution owned by people of color. If not for women there would never have been created the first AME Church in Los Angles while Juneteenth was yet trying to find enslaved black folks in the West.

If not for women, there would be no hair care products for us; no NAACP for us; and no creams and lotions for our body care. If not for women, there would be no new and improved South! While European Americans were dreaming, planning, and working outside their homes in industry, manufacturing, and economics, it was black women who were raising their children, cleaning their homes, and making sure that a decent meal was on their tables.

"Who can find a woman of virtue?" We remember the women who are responsible for our being here today. When we dare to recall the struggles, the sacrifices, and the self-giving, self-denying, and self-killing ways in which women, who many called Mama, Ma Dear, Big Mama, and Granny, wore themselves out to give us life today, we have the answer to the ancient question. Clearly, our perspective, our answers, nor our lives were taken into consideration when that question in Proverbs was written.

The Bible is a record of stories told, according to the needs, the personalities, and the position of Jewish men. In every culture, the status of men is uplifted before that of women. So we must approach the reading of scriptures with this fact of male dominance in mind. If you would dare to look at the first book of the Bible, you will find another story outlined that does not look like the one in chapter 2.

This book of beginnings is not history, as we know it. There were no human beings to record the creation. We know that the beginning is not simply some scientific myth according to Darwin's theory of evolution, where we emerged from the creation of the apes. Therefore, we are left to infer that the Genesis account of creation is a tale of revelation, handed down by oral tradition.

Every culture enjoys a good story. There are millions of creation stories told by every culture under the sun. We had to learn about the

Greek gods and goddesses and all of the Roman myths while we were in school. We all remember hearing some form of the story of Pandora and her box, which is another version of the creation. However, the text from Genesis 2 that is before us today is an inspired creation of time's birth, as told by Moses, the friend of God.

Turn with me to Genesis, chapter 1. It begins, "In the beginning, God." Elohim, the strong and mighty one, is known as *Bereshith*, the same who emerged from eternity for the commencement of time. And this *Bara*, interpreted as the Highest Being to be reverenced, by word of mouth, from *ex nihilo*, out of nothing, produced everything we now call the heavens and the earth. The heavens, where God, the Trinity, and the ever-praising angelic host dwell, and earth, a terrestrial globe with both atmospheric elements and firmament, were both created by the One who holds eternity!

There was chaos, desolation, and no population in the formless, lifeless, shapeless, objectless, and tenantless form of matter until Elohim, the Creator, spoke. In the midst of a shrouded, thick gloom, with no light, no order, and no life form to be seen, the Spirit of God moved upon the face of the waters. It was the *ruach* of Elohim, the life-giving Spirit, with wind and breath that began the initial movement that advanced slowly and began a great transformation. Out from eternity, God stepped and God spoke. It was the beginning of time. The evolution of the cosmos was accomplished by a series of divine formative works that extended over a six-day period. And more powerfully on ten different times we read the words: "And God said . . ."

God spoke and every time the divine essence breathed out a word, it was followed by instantaneous movement. For the Living Word is creative all by itself. God spoke and we see the beginning of light separating darkness. God spoke and we get air and water. God spoke and then we see dry land and plant life. God spoke and there are greater and lesser celestial lights; followed by fowl and fish. God spoke and the world received the creation of the animal kingdom.

Everything possessed the potency of life—the ability to reproduce itself. And God said, "It is good."

Now, everything was ready for the *magnum opus,* which was to close the creative labor of the Sovereign and be the foreshadowing of the marriage between Jesus and his bride, the church. There was a concilium among the Trinity as the construction of this new creature was considered. "Let us make humankind in our image, according to our likeness," states chapter 1, verse 26. They will have dominion over the earth, declares that same verse. The following verse, 27, says, "So God created humankind in his image, in the image of God, he created them; male and female, he created them."

In verse 28, God blessed them. And God said to them, "Be fruitful and multiply, and fill the earth and subdue it; and have dominion over the fish of the sea and over the birds of the air and over every living thing that moves upon the earth. Verse 31 concludes with the full cosmos being given as a glorious benediction, "God saw every thing that he had made, and indeed, it was very good." If we stop right here, we find that woman, the symbol of the church of God, was given, along with her mate, the body image, the reason, the beauty, the intelligent speech, erect stature, a soul, and a moral nature at the same time. They both were created spiritual beings, with moral integrity and holiness, and with free agency, and they were given dominion over creatures.

They were both given rule and supremacy. Three times it's said that God created them, male and female on the sixth day. The Creator pronounced that both of them were very, exceedingly good, beautiful and excellent, without fault, blemish, or sin. Here, in chapter 1, it's both the male and the female that are created at the same time and given equality by God. In the creation of the human couple, we find God's resolution to have a last, final, and even a greatest work. In the creation we see God's forethought. All else was executed with Word instantaneously. But there was divine handiwork involved in the making of Adam and Eve. They needed personal care and attention. There was divine delight in fashioning them in the divine image.

This couple was kin to the Godhead. This couple was made in heavenly image and likeness. This couple was given the *imago Dei*, or a resemblance to the divine Image. Both the man and the woman were given personality, purity, power, intellect, and wisdom to become representatives of God—visible embodiments of the Supreme as they walked among the lower creation.

When the creation was complete, God instituted the Sabbath day for rest. Both creation stories agree on this fact. However, we have several differences that we must recognize. In the first creation story of Genesis 1:11, we see that God produces vegetation at will; in Genesis 2:4–5, vegetation depends upon rain, mists, and agricultural labor. In Genesis 1:7, the earth emerges from the waters and is saturated with moisture. In the second story, earth appears dry, sterile, and sandy. And then there is the first story where man and woman are created together, while in Genesis 2:7, the man is created first with the woman being later extracted from his body in verse 22. In the first story, Adam bears the image of God. In the second story, his earth-formed body is animated by the breath of life and he is placed in Eden to cultivate and to guard it. In the first story, the birds and the beasts are created before the humans. In the second story, man is created before the beasts in order to name them. You must choose what story best fits your theology. And we are forced to deal with the differences. We must wrestle as well with the woman wisdom's creation story in Proverbs. (Please read Proverbs 8:22–31.)

What we have is an internal unity between all stories. God was the creator, and we are the creation. What we have is a divine bestowment of life from mere dust, in a garden environment where all that is needed is to wait for the arrival of humans. What we find is the startling fact that the church is a divinely prepared female creature, woman, exceptional in her glory and prophetic—a woman called Wisdom. Wisdom is both stimulating our hope and stimulating our faith while being assigned our work to be fruitful and multiply. She is God's most responsible servant!

There is a four-part river in the garden that corresponds to the four Gospels of Jesus Christ. It is the gospel that spreads hope. It is the gospel that brings healing. It is the gospel that sheds light and gives life. And, it is the good news of the gospel that enables us to rejoice in our hope in Jesus Christ. In the garden, there is a tree whose fruit is good for the healing of the nations. In the garden was placed a man who remained sinless and perfect. And in the Garden of Eden was placed a woman with a marriage contract. "Therefore a man leaves his father and his mother and clings to his wife, and they become one flesh" (Gen. 2:24).

Ephesians 5:22 picks up this marriage covenant as it begins, "Wives, be subject to your husbands as you are to the Lord." Verses 25–27 say, "Husbands, love your wives just as Christ loved the church and gave himself up for her, in order to make her holy by cleansing her with the washing of water by the word, so as to present the church to himself in splendor, without a spot or wrinkle or anything of the kind—yes, so that she may be holy and without blemish."

Finally, we arrive at the conclusion of the matter in verses 31–32: "For this reason a man will leave his father and mother and be joined to his wife, and the two will become one flesh. This is a great mystery, and I am applying it to Christ and the church." The creation of Adam and Eve is the story of Christ and his bride. The creation of Adam and Eve is the symbolic message that we have for the act of marriage being such a holy covenant, a life-giving act between a man and woman. The creation of Adam and Eve, Jesus being the second Adam of the Spirit, and the church being called woman, is a permanent and visible reminder of just how much God loved, valued, and made significant the role of every woman.

As we look at that woman in Proverbs 31, we can begin to better understand this portrait of a woman who is virtuous, industrious, organized, outreaching, managing, overseeing, and including all with needs within her grasp. This is not a passage to make us work ourselves to death. This is a passage that says, this woman, called the church, needs to get it together! This woman, called the church, is filled with gifted, talented, wise people who seek to fulfill the mission and the ministry of the Bridegroom. This woman, called the church, is expected to be about the business of being called excellent; of being praised by the city; of being admired by her people, her community, and her offspring. This woman, called the church, is being watched over by her spouse, because she is loved. She is appreciated. She is well applauded for her industry, her creativity, and her vision. She's strong in God and in the power of the Holy Spirit to accomplish far more than we, as single, independent women can ever think or imagine! For her name is woman and she is the church of Jesus Christ as a community gathered! Her name is woman and she is the bride of the coming Bridegroom.

The church, a woman, has so many of our natural and human tendencies. So, if we would be really honest and look at our local congregation through the lens of a woman, we can better understand the primary concerns that are holding us back. As you deal with this church, this woman, take a few notes so that you can flesh this out later. One of the most destructive habits that women have is worry. We spend too much time obsessing over stuff that never happens. While a woman's greatest joy tends to come from giving, the reality is that we give away all of our stuff for free. Our greatest loss is living in a secondhand manner and inferiority mode rather than living up to our God-given self-respect.

The most satisfying work of the average woman is that of helping others. We, however, will help without being willing to ask for help when we need it. We cannot be both independent and interdependent at the same time. But God called the church to community and interdependency. There are no super solo stars in the church of God! Surely the ugliest personality trait that any woman can ever exhibit is that of being selfish, trying to keep all of what she's got for herself. And the average woman of color has a tendency to not share either her burden or her power, even though Jesus gave power away.

The most endangered species among women are those who prove to be dedicated leaders. We know how to do so very many things and to do them so well. But, we don't know how to train others to take our place in order for the responsibilities to be carried on when we are gone. We need to recognize and to cultivate the reality that our greatest natural resource is our youth. They need our attention, teaching, and instruction today, not tomorrow. They think that they know. But we know that they don't know, and we need to be about the business of paying attention to them and drawing them into active ministry.

We need to believe and to give to each other, more often, that greatest "shot in the arm"—a word of encouragement. If what we have to say to each other is not to build up their labor, we need to learn how to keep it to ourselves! The gift of encouragement is sadly missing in the Christian church. The greatest problem that we need to overcome is the demon that we know as fear. For we talk with double tongue when we declare, "I can do all things through Christ" and yet fail to take action.

The most crippling disease that any woman can possess is excuses. The most dangerous woman is a gossiper. The deadliest weapon of every woman is her tongue. The worst thing for any woman to be without is hope. The most worthless emotion that any woman can have is self-pity. The world's most incredible computer is a woman's brain. The two most power-filled words of any woman are "I can!" The greatest asset given to woman is her faith. The most beautiful attire a woman can wear is her own authentic SMILE! The most prized possession of a woman is her integrity. She stands on her word. The most powerful channel of communication that each woman can use is prayer. The most contagious spirit that a woman can utilize is her enthusiasm, while the most important thing in a woman's life is her relationship with Jesus Christ. And the most powerful force in any woman's life is love.

The church of the Living God was created by divine design. She is both a gift and a present to a dying world. Jesus gave his life and died for her. The Holy Spirit lives inside of her. Whosoever will can enter into her sacred space and receive life. For she is good and very good, and, her name is Woman! She is God's most responsible servant! And that's all good!

LOOKING OUT FOR YOUR OWN BEST INTEREST

Test yourself to see how you fare with the stewardship of your life.[1]

Christian Stewardship

1. Do you know for sure that you have eternal life?
2. Do you pray and read your Bible daily?
3. Have you won anyone to Christ in the past twelve months?
4. Are you making consistent contributions of your time and talents to ministries in your local church?

Stewardship in Your Profession

1. Do you give your boss a full day's work?
2. Do you get to work on time?
3. Do you complete assignments on time?
4. When you begin your workday, do you know the primary tasks that need completion that day?

Stewardship in Finances

1. Do you know how much money you need to pay off all your debts?
2. Do you know your net worth?

3. Do you live by a budget?
4. Have your bank transactions been free of returned checks for the past twenty-four months?
5. Do you tithe (10 percent of your income)?
6. Do you save a set amount of money regularly?
7. Are you free of bills for which you are a cosigner?
8. Do you have good credit?
9. Can you go freely in public without worrying about seeing someone to whom you owe money that you have not paid?
10. Do you report all income on your income taxes?
11. Are your income tax deductions legitimate?
12. If you are undercharged for a purchase do you return the money that you should have been charged?
13. Could you handle a $1500 emergency right now without borrowing the money?
14. Can you pay off all of your credit card balances within ninety days?
15. Do you have a will, estate plan, or other strategy for the distribution of assets in the event of your death?

Medical/Physical Stewardship

1. Do you visit your doctor for regular medical checkups?
2. Are you compliant with medications your doctor has prescribed?
3. Do you exercise regularly?
4. Do you control your weight?
5. Do you eat a well-balanced diet?
6. Do you get enough rest?
7. Are you free of dangerous health habits such as smoking, drinking, and drug use?

Family Stewardship

1. Do you spend quality time with your children?
2. Do you spend quality time with your spouse?

3. Do you teach your children to be clean, orderly, and organized, to get enough rest, to eat properly, etc.?

4. Can you name your great grandparents?

Personal Stewardship

1. Do you have a written mission statement in which you have clearly defined your personal values and vision?

2. Are your thoughts and conversation free of vulgarity, perversion, and profanity?

3. Do you communicate with others to inform them if you are going to miss a meeting, be late, or in any way failing to meet their expectations?

4. Is your car clean and well-kept?

5. Is your laundry and wardrobe always in order so that you avoid delays caused by not finding anything to wear to an event?

6. Do you keep your schedule with your barber or beautician, thereby avoiding bad hair days?

7. Is your house clean and organized?

8. Have you repaired or replaced all broken home appliances?

9. Do you return phone calls in a timely manner?

10. Do you return borrowed items free of coffee stains, fingerprints, grease, and other defacing marks?

11. Is your closet free of clutter and items you do not wear?

12. Can you locate operations manuals for your car, tape recorder, stereo, refrigerator, computer, cellular phone, beeper, fax machine, air conditioner, washer and dryer, microwave, stove, and other appliances?

13. Are you current in your car maintenance schedule?

Stewardship of Relationships

1. Are you friendly and courteous towards others?

2. Do you avoid gossip and negativity?

3. Do you restore harmony in broken relationships or make every effort to avoid extended periods of discord between you and others?

LETTER GRADES	NUMERICAL SCORE	WRITTEN ASSESSMENT
A	45–50	Excellent Steward
B	40–45	Good Steward
C	35–39	Fair Steward
D	30–34	Poor Steward
F	25–	Desperately Poor Steward

"A slack hand causes poverty, but the hand of the diligent makes rich" (Prov. 10:4).

12

STANDING FAITH?

The Stewardship of Faith-Filled Living

W hen the world seems to defeat you and you are sick with the disorder, the violence, the terror, the war on the streets; when the earth seems to be chaos, say to yourself, "Jesus died and rose again on purpose to save, and his salvation is already with us." I can stand on this faith! Every newly opened leper-hospital or HIV/AIDS clinic is an act of faith in the resurrection. Every peace treaty and conflict resolved is an act of faith in the resurrection. Every commitment agreed upon is an act of faith in the resurrection. When you forgive your enemy. When you feed the hungry. When you defend the weak you believe in the resurrection. When you have the courage to marry. When you build your home to welcome the newly born child. When you bury a parent, a sibling, or a child, you believe in the resurrection. When you awake at peace in the morning. When you sing to the rising sun. When you go to work with joy. And when you live and pray, in faith, believing and acting, you believe in the resurrection.[1]

Easter Sunday is actually the birthday of God's church. Easter Sunday begins a new and different church or Christian year for us. It's a sacred time when Christians start all over again, celebrating the power and living afresh by the power of God that raised Jesus from the dead. For it is this same power that raises us from every down place, every down situation, every down circumstance and even from every trying-to-take-us-down individual! Easter is our theme song that says, "Still I rise!" And still I stand! Each Easter is a promise that Jesus will be back to take us "home" with him. Each Easter is another symbol that our real "beginning" in eternity is already underway.

Lent and Easter of 2004 will go down in my memory forever. I have had to ask myself if I really did believe that Jesus died and rose again from the dead. I have had to wrestle and to struggle with my faith in a resurrection and eternal life. For the subject of resurrection is no longer objective for me. My youngest son, Grelon, died the week before Easter, and I had to ask myself if I really did believe that Jesus rose. That Lent and Easter season will remain alive with me for as long as I live. For Easter is no longer just the occasion to buy spring decor, locate an Easter basket, and purchase a new outfit. I have had to stand and look down on the physical tent/tabernacle/house of my own flesh and blood and determine if I really did believe that Jesus got up one early Easter morning. Grelon Renard Everett was forty years old. He had suffered the debilitating effects of severe diabetes that resulted in kidney failure, legal blindness, and a hole in one foot for five years.

The only thing that did not get affected by the ugly ravages of these past years was his faith in Jesus Christ. "Mama, don't worry. Jesus promised me that I would not go blind." He didn't go blind. "Mama, don't worry. Jesus promised me that I would not have to have an amputation." He didn't have his foot amputated. As I stood in the morgue that day, to anoint Grelon's head with oil, to look upon his peaceful face, and to touch is lovely hair, I felt with certainty that Jesus really did get up from the dead. I was affirmed that my child was not dead, but had simply slipped from the bondage of a damaged body into eternal life. I could release that empty tent back to God, knowing that Grelon is now whole and without pain. Mel Gibson's *The Passion of Christ,* has caused us all to rethink the steps that led to Easter. The picture is rated "R" for its violence. My preaching sister, Deborah Shumake of Detroit, sent me the following explanation.

> Let's see if it makes this Easter more clear for us. The "R" of course, in the movie is because of the violence, the gore and the blood that we are forced to watch. According to Hollywood's standards, in movie terms, "R," stands for *restricted.* But in the reality of the life and death of Jesus Christ, the "R" stands for *relevant,* for *realistic,* for it *really* happened for a *reason.* It was because we were *rebellious,* we needed a *redeemer,* we needed to be *reconciled,* we needed to be *recovered* and we needed to be *regenerated.* Jesus needed to be *rejected* so that we could have a *relationship* not just a *religion.* The "R" is to *remind* us what Jesus did to *remove* our sin, to *render* Satan powerless and to *rescue* us from eternity in hell. The "R" is to show that Jesus was *responsible* for giving us eternal *rest.* As a result of his death Jesus *retired* our debt. The "R" rating means that some will be *repulsed,* some will *refuse* to believe, some will be *reluctant,* and some will think that we are *ridiculous* in believing that a death was *required.* The "R" means that the *result* of sin has been *reversed.* Now, through faith in Christ, our *reward* is eternity and we are now *righteous* before God because we have *received* him as the *ruler* of our soul. What a *revolutionary* and *radical* solution to *redeem* all of humankind." (Author unknown)

May every Sunday, a symbol of Easter, be the beginning of our radical witness to a needy world that Jesus got up just to live in us! Each "Easter Sunday" is another occasion to be reminded that we are yet responsible for the stewardship of faith-filled living in the world. It is our duty to tell those who are dead to the news of new life that there is a reality to the True, the Risen, and the Living Christ in God. For the "official" Easter, with its gorgeous white lilies, bright colorful tulips, and "must-have" Easter eggs, says as our reality, new life has come, death, sin, the grave, and coldness have been banished because Jesus Christ reigns—world without end.

The Apostle Paul ministered among the new congregations in Thessalonica for only a short time. In his letter writing activities, however, he spent much time teaching them. Because they were beginning to establish a new religious order, a different way of life, and an established method of serving God that was not "ordained and sanctified" by the leadership of the day, they suffered much persecution. They were not a politically correct congregation. They were simply people who had heard, believed, and received the Easter message and were hated because of it. So Paul wrote to encourage them, to thank them for being faithful, and to exhort them to both prayer and community as they witnessed to their new life.

The Urban Ministries' *Sunday School Annual* gives us the following admonition about our corporate worship: "Worship is both personal and corporate. In corporate worship, God communes with us through the reading of Scriptures, preaching, sharing of sacraments and ordinances, prayers and music. We respond to God through our praise, adoration, thanksgiving, sharing our time, gifts and resources and in prayer. In both corporate and in our personal, private worship, we demonstrate our belief and our faith in the Eternal One. . . . Our expressions of praise in prayers and songs affirm the Eternal Creator's past, present and future activity in our lives."[2]

Saying and singing our prayers is so essential to develop a faith-filled life of stewardship and worship. Saying and singing our prayers is the only way that we can stand, firmly rooted in God's promises through the storms of life. Saying and singing our prayers is the only way that keeps us connected to the All Knowing Sovereign of the universe, who reigns supreme! Saying and singing our prayers, whether through sacred music, hymns, anthems, spirituals, metered songs, inspirational gospel, quartet gospel, contemporary gospel, praise chorus, or chorale responses, are all ways to help us walk through life's storms with our heads held high! If you want to stand strong in a storm, ask God to send you a song to linger in your spirit!

I am liturgically "correct," which means that I follow the lectionary and know what each season of the Christian year means and needs in the way of corporate worship. So, on that Easter Sunday after Grelon died, I knew what was "appropriate" to sing in the Sunday worship. Yet, way down in my spirit, my soul, the seat of my being, I just needed to hear, "I need thee, oh, I need thee. Every hour, I need thee. O, bless me now my Savior, I come to thee."[3]

Thank God for one of our lead psalmists, Brother George Lowe, who heard my cry and took us there before we began the "lectionary correct Easter music." For it was the first Sunday since my son's memorial, and I had to have strength to make it through. I prayed in song. Many others present in worship had the very same need. And Jesus Christ rose in us because we prayed. We truly experienced resurrection!

Paul gave God thanks, always mentioning the saints in Thessalonica in his prayers. Paul knew that they were praying for him. They supported him monetarily. So he writes: "We always give thanks to God for all of you and mention you in our prayers, constantly remembering before our God . . . your work of faith and labor of love, and steadfastness of hope in our Lord Jesus Christ" (1 Thess. 1:2–3). Paul knew their circumstances and realized how they were sacrificing to be living witnesses of the Risen Christ. Since Grelon's death, this has also become my testimony and my prayer to God. For *you* have been so great, so loving, so generous, and so kind that it's been overwhelming. I believe in resurrection because I have seen and experienced Christ in *you!* Like too many young black men, Grelon had no insurance. We had to pay all of his expenses from our personal funds. *You* have paid his bills, in full!

You sent Giraurd, our grandson, on the Historically Black College/ University tour by your generosity after Grelon's death. *You* fed us, both family and friends, with your hospitality and outreach to us. *You* have traveled to visit, sent cards, called, and brought so much food, so many plants and flowers until we have had to share them with others. *You* have paid for Grelon's worship service bulletins and gone beyond the call of duty with his obituary being placed in the Gary, Indiana, and Lansing and Grand Rapids, Michigan, newspapers. *You* have sent me stamps. And one of God's shocking surprises was that *you* even put "Thank You" cards on my front porch the very day that I ran out! We, all of Grelon's family, give thanks to God always for *you* all! We could not have made it without *you!*

"Sure, people need Jesus, but most of the time, what they really need is for someone to be Jesus to them."[4] *You* have been the Risen and Living Christ to us on this new journey of faith-filled living. We can never repay your love. But we can, we do, and we will pray for *you*, for it is you who have helped us to keep standing in this storm. We thank each and every one of *you!* Now I ask that *you* find someone around you who is bending from one of life's storm and be the resurrected Jesus to that person. Hurting people are everywhere. Just open your eyes and see! And, if it's *you* who needs someone, just holla . . . I declare that the saints, the real people of God, will come!

Once again, I thank God for this rare opportunity to share with you through the printed pages. I "feel" you. I'm praying for you. I'm committed to living so that I can continue to learn life's lessons and to pass on my "education" with you to encourage you to hang in there! For life is difficult! But the God who called us is more than able to conquer and to vanquish every difficulty! For with God there are no impossibilities, only pathways to possibilities for us to discover!

To God be all the glory! We will keep searching. We will continue to discover. And I promise that we will continue to share. Thanks for being on the journey with me. Let's covenant to grow on!

And now unto the One, the Only Sovereign Christ, who is able to keep us from falling, and to present us as without fault before God's throne, be glory, and honor and power, dominion and might, world without end and forevermore as we live lives of committed stewardship and receive, in eternity, our just rewards!

This year . . . live holy! Laugh often! And love with flair and extravagance! You can reach me at: Rev. Dr. Linda H. Hollies, Spiritual Director/Pastoral Counselor, WomanSpace (616-776-9706). WomanSpace is a sacred place for God's bodacious woman! Saving sisters, one woman at a time! Join us!

NOTES

PREFACE

1. Phenessa A. Gray, *My Soul's Surrender* (Bloomington, Ind.: AuthorHouse, 2002), 3. Used by permission.

CHAPTER 2

1. www.economist.com/market/display/story/cfm?story_id3625027.

2. Mary Bellis, "The History of Money and Credit Cards," www.inventors.about.com/library/inventors/blmoney.htm; http://www.cardpay.net/creditcardhistory.htm.

CHAPTER 4

1. Daniel Iverson, "Spirit of the Living God," 1926, © 1935, 1963 Moody Bible Institute.

CHAPTER 8

1. Renita Weems, *Showing Mary* (West Bloomfield, Michigan: Walk Worthy Books, 2002).

2. Gwynne Forster, *When Twilight Comes*, (New York: Dafina Books, 2002).

3. Alfred Ackley, "He Lives," 1933, © 1933, renewed 1961 The Rodeheaver Co.

CHAPTER 9

1. Terrie Williams, *A Plentiful Harvest*, (New York: Warner Books, 2002), 119–21.

CHAPTER 10

1. Terrie Williams, *A Plentiful Harvest*, (New York: Warner Books, 2002), 137–39.

CHAPTER 11

1. Vernita Williams, "The Stewardship Test," *Precious Times Magazine*, vol. 2, issue 1, (Winter 2004), 42–43. Used by permission of the author.

CHAPTER 12

1. From Carlo Carretto, *Blessed Are You Who Believed*, trans. Barbara Wall (Maryknoll, N.Y.: Orbis Books, 1994), cited in *Christianity Today*, 40, no. 4.

2. *The Sunday School Annual on the International Sunday School Lesson* (Calumet City, Ill.: Urban Ministries, 2004), 240.

3. Annie S. Hawks, "I Need Thee Every Hour," 1872.

4. Reuben Welch, quoted in Robert Benson, *The Body Broken* (New York: Doubleday, 2003). A Soul Boosters quote found at www.spirituality health.com/newsh/items/soulbooster/item_8361.html.

Other books from The Pilgrim Press

ON THEIR WAY TO WONDERFUL
A Journey with Ruth and Naomi
Linda H. Hollies

0-8298-1604-6/paper/130 pages/$18.00

This resource is an exploration of multicultural marriage (Ruth and Boaz) as well as diversity and racism in Scripture (Ruth, a Moabite whom God allows to enter the forbidden Jewish bloodline). Women will relate to this book as it touches on issues that impact their lives, such as making critical decisions, handling relationships, and renewal of self and soul.

BODACIOUS WOMANIST WISDOM
Linda H. Hollies

0-8298-1529-5/paper/144 pages/$18.00

Hollies takes a look at the "bodaciousness" of women of color through biblical stories of specific women such as the "bent-over woman" in Luke 13, Queen Esther, Mary, and other unnamed biblical women. Each chapter ends with a "Woman Wisdom Speaks" quote from Scripture and "Womanist Wisdom" and "Bodacious Woman" words.

JESUS AND THOSE BODACIOUS WOMEN
Life Lessons from One Sister to Another
Linda H. Hollies

0-8298-1246-6/paper/224 pages/$11.95

Linda Hollies serves up new spins on the stories of biblical women. From Eve to Mary Magdalene, portraits of the bodaciousness of the many matriarchs of the Christian tradition will prove to be blessings for readers. Study questions and suggestions providing examples of courage and of how to grow in faith and spirituality, are included at the end of each chapter.

TAKING BACK MY YESTERDAYS

Lessons in Forgiving and Moving Forward with Your Life

LINDA H. HOLLIES

0-8298-1208-3/paper/192 pages/$10.95

"A must read book! Linda Hollies has successfully combined personal honesty and solid biblical storytelling to teach us how to forgive and let go of yesterday. . . . The prayers will inspire you. The principles will encourage you. The psalms will direct your path." Iyanla Vanzant, author Acts of Faith, talk show host of IYANLA.

MOTHER GOOSE MEETS A WOMAN CALLED WISDOM

A Short Course in the Art of Self-Determination

LINDA H. HOLLIES

0-8298-1348-9/cloth/142 pages/$21.95

Fairy tales will never be the same! Hollies retells classic fairy tales with a decidedly spiritual spin. She provides a guidebook for women at the crossroads of their lives while looking at biblical women. The result is a biblical approach to practicing the art of self-determination.

PILGRIM PRAYERS FOR GRANDMOTHERS RAISING GRANDCHILDREN

LINDA H. HOLLIES

0-8298-1490-6/paper/128 pages/$10.00

This book will inspire grandmothers and give them the encouragement and comfort they need for the unique journey of raising their grandchildren.

VASHTI'S VICTORY

And Other Biblical Women Resisting Injustice

LAVERNE MCCAIN GILL

0-8298-1521-X/paper/128 pp./$16.00

Gill examines and discusses six Bible stories using the "Justice Reading Strategy" she employed in her book, *Daughters of Dignity: African Women of the Bible and the Virtues of Black Womanhood.* She features the women surrounding Moses, Michal, and the daughters of Zelophehad along with others and compares them to contemporary women who have resisted injustices.

To order these or any other books from The Pilgrim Press call or write to:

THE PILGRIM PRESS
700 PROSPECT AVENUE EAST
CLEVELAND, OHIO 44115-1100

PHONE ORDERS: 1-800-537-3394 ▪ FAX ORDERS: 216-736-2206

Please include shipping charges of $5.00 for the first book and $0.75 for each additional book. Or order from our web sites at www.thepilgrimpress.com and www.ucpress.com.

Prices subject to change without notice.